# The Essentials Of Theory U

## Core Principles And Applications

C. Otto Scharmer

**16**

EasyRead Large

RHYW

# Copyright Page from the Original Book

## The Essentials of Theory U

Berrett-Koehler Publishers, Inc.
1333 Broadway, Suite 1000
Oakland, CA 94612-1921
Tel: (510) 817-2277, Fax: (510) 817-2278
www.bkconnection.com

Ordering information for print editions
*Quantity sales.* Special discounts are available on quantity purchases by corporations, associations, and others. For details, contact the "Special Sales Department" at the Berrett-Koehler address above.
*Individual sales.* Berrett-Koehler publications are available through most bookstores. They can also be ordered directly from Berrett-Koehler: Tel: (800) 929-2929; Fax: (802) 864-7626; www.bkconnection.com
*Orders for college textbook/course adoption use.* Please contact Berrett-Koehler: Tel: (800) 929-2929; Fax: (802) 864-7626.
Distributed to the U.S. trade and internationally by Penguin Random House Publisher Services.

Berrett-Koehler and the BK logo are registered trademarks of Berrett-Koehler Publishers, Inc.

First Edition
Paperback print edition ISBN 978-1-5230-9440-0
PDF e-book ISBN 978-1-5230-9441-7
IDPF e-book ISBN 978-1-5230-9442-4

2018-1

Book producer: Westchester Publishing Services

Text designer: Lynn L'Heureux

Cover designer: Richard Adelson

Interior illustration: Kelvy Bird

# TABLE OF CONTENTS

# Other books by the Author include

*Theory U: Leading from the Future as it Emerges 1st Edition*

*Leading from the Emerging Future: From Ego-system to Eco-system Economies*

*Prescence: Human Purpose and the Field of the Future*

*To*

*the emerging movement of people who*
*bridge the three major divides of our time:*
*the ecological, the social, and the spiritual divide.*

# Preface

Ten years after the original publication of Theory U in 2006, my publisher approached me about writing this book. Somewhat more politely than this, he said: "Okay, *Theory U* has been selling well. But frankly, we have no idea why. It is almost impossible to read. Five hundred pages, dozens of tables, hundreds of footnotes—it embodies everything that a publisher would tell you *not* to do." Then he suggested, "Why don't you, for a change, now write a book that is readable—shorter, more accessible, and updated?"

I probably seemed a bit offended. When he saw that, he quickly pointed out how a couple of other authors, whom I happen to admire, had done what he was suggesting: First, write comprehensively about what you have invented, and then in the next book explain it in a more accessible way. The book you are now holding is the result.

I hope it will serve you well. By providing this introduction to Theory

U—an awareness-based method for changing systems—I try to answer the question: How do we learn in the face of disruption? How do we learn from the future as it emerges?

Theory U blends systems thinking, innovation, and leading change—from the viewpoint of an evolving human consciousness. Drawing on the Massachusetts Institute of Technology (MIT) tradition of action research and learning by doing, Theory U has evolved over two decades of experimentation and refinement by a vibrant global community of practitioners. At its core, Theory U comprises three main elements:

1. A framework for seeing the blind spot of leadership and systems change
2. A method for implementing awareness-based change: process, principles, practices
3. A new narrative for evolutionary societal change: updating our mental and institutional operating systems (OS) in all of society's sectors

Part I explores the framework and main ideas of Theory U (chapters 1–4). It illuminates the most important blind spot in leadership today: the "interior condition" from which we operate.

Part II describes the process, principles, and practices of Theory U (chapter 5). It showcases practical methods and tools for change makers. The focus is on building the collective capacity to *shift the inner place* from which we operate.

Part III introduces a new narrative for profound evolutionary change in society (chapters 6–7). What does it take to redesign societies in ways that address the pressing challenges of our time? What does it take to apply the power of mindfulness to the transformation of the collective system? This part of the book outlines a framework for updating the "operating systems" of our educational institutions, our economies, and our democracies. This framework applies the core concepts of Theory U to the transformation of capitalism.

Theory U integrates these methods and lineages for effecting change:

- Action research and organizational learning in the tradition of Peter Senge, Ed Schein, Donald Schön, Chris Argyris, and Kurt Lewin
- Design thinking in the tradition of Tim Brown and Dave Kelly
- Mindfulness, cognition science, and phenomenology in the tradition of Francisco Varela, Jon Kabat-Zinn, Tanja Singer, Arthur Zajonc, and David Bohm
- Civil society movements in the tradition of Martin Luther King Jr., Nelson Mandela, Mahatma Gandhi, and millions of others who are mobilizing change in their local contexts

# Theory U Leadership: Cultivate the Social Field

At its core, Theory U makes a distinction between the different ways that action and attention come into the world. *I pay attention this way, therefore it emerges that way.* Or, as the late CEO of Hanover Insurance, Bill O'Brien, put it: "The success of an intervention depends on the interior condition of the intervener."

Theory U draws our attention to the *blind spot* in leadership today: the "interior conditions," the sources from which we operate both individually and collectively.

Since I grew up on a farm, I like to compare our interior condition to a field. Each field has two dimensions: one that is visible, what's growing above the surface; and one that is invisible, what's beneath the surface—that is, the quality of the soil.

The same distinction applies to social fields. We can see what people do, the practical outcomes that they accomplish in the visible realm. But we rarely pay attention to the deeper root condition: the *source* and interior condition *from* which we operate. Theory U draws our attention to that blind spot—to the invisible source dimension of the social field, to the quality of relationships that we have to each other, to the system, and to ourselves.

Theory U identifies four different ways (or sources from) that action and attention come into the world. They arise from a quality of awareness that is (1) habitual, (2) ego-systemic, (3) empathic-relational, or (4) generative eco-systemic.

The essence of leadership is to become aware of our blind spot (these interior conditions or sources) and then **to shift the inner place from which we operate** as required by the situations we face. This means that our job as leaders and change makers is **to cultivate the soil of the social field.** The *social field* consists of the relationships among individuals, groups, and systems that give rise to patterns of thinking, conversing, and organizing, which in turn produce practical results.

Social fields are like social systems—but they are seen *from within,* from their interior condition. To shift from a social *system* perspective to a social *field* perspective, we have to become aware of our blind spot, the source level from which our attention and our actions originate. That source level fundamentally affects the quality of leading, learning, and listening.

The problem with leadership today is that most people think of it as being made up of individuals, with one person at the top. But if we see leadership as the capacity of a system to co-sense and co-shape the future, then we realize that all leadership is distributed—it needs to include everyone. To develop collective capacity, everyone must act as a steward for the larger eco-system. To do that in a more reliable, distributed, and intentional way, we need:

- A social grammar: a language
- A social technology: methods and tools
- And a new narrative of social change

The grammar of the social field is spelled out in Part I. The method, an awareness-based social technology, is spelled out in Part II. In Part III, they are incorporated into a narrative of societal and civilizational renewal.

Theory U revolves around a core process of co-sensing and co-shaping emerging future possibilities. But it is much more than that. The grammar and the method outlined in this book work as a matrix, not as a linear process. Some of the leadership capacities that are at the heart of the U method include:

- **Suspension and wonder:** Only in the suspension of judgment can we open ourselves up to wonder. Wonder is about noticing that there is a world beyond our patterns of downloading.
- **Co-sensing:** You must go to places of most potential yourself because it is in these connections that the seeds of the future come into the world. Connect with these places with your mind and heart wide open.
- **The power of intention:** The power of "intention" is key. In all presencing work, the deeper intention is the opposite of corporate indoctrination. It is about increasing, not decreasing, your range of possibilities. It is about strengthening your sources of self in a world that otherwise tends to tear us apart. It is about making you aware of your own sources of curiosity, compassion, and courage.
- **Co-creating:** Explore the future by doing, by building small landing strips for the future that wants to emerge.

- **Container building:** Create new holding spaces that activate the generative social field.

The problem with our current societal eco-systems is the broken feedback loop between the parts and the whole. Theory U offers a method for **relinking the parts and the whole** by making it possible for the **system to sense and see itself.** When that happens, the collective consciousness begins to shift from **ego-system awareness** to **eco-system awareness**—from a **silo view** to a **systems view.**

The Theory U methods and tools enable groups to do this on the level of the collective. For example, Social Presencing Theater makes it possible for a group of stakeholders in a system to sense and see themselves—both individually and collectively—by **bending the beam of observation back** onto the observer.

This matters because **energy follows attention.** Wherever we put our attention as leader, educator, parent, etc.—that is where the energy of the team will go. The moment we see the quality of attention shifting from ego to eco, from *me* to *we,* that is when the deeper conditions of the field open up, when the **generative social field** is being activated.

My work with these and other methods of change over the past two-plus decades boils down to this: The quality of results achieved by any system is a function of the quality of awareness that people in these systems operate from. In three words: **Form follows consciousness.**

# Acknowledgments

While a new methodology for leading awareness-based systems change is at the heart of this book, it is also about the journey of the self—in this case, *myself,* a kid who grew up on a farm, became an activist in social movements, and then started rethinking economics and building learning infrastructures in teams, in organizations, and on the societal level. This journey has of course been embedded in a whole web of relationships that co-created the work described in this book.

My heartfelt thanks goes out to the global network of partners and collaborators who helped (1) to articulate this framework, (2) to refine the methodology, and (3) to co-create a narrative and movement that, given today's challenges, has never been more timely.

A deep bow to the co-creators of the Presencing Institute (PI):

The co-founders

- Katrin Kaufer, for pioneering new capacity-building environments in values-based banks by blending the intentional use of capital with presencing practices
- Arawana Hayashi, for creating *Social Presencing Theater,* a new method and art form for embodied knowing in social systems
- Kelvy Bird, for creating the method of *generative scribing* that embodies presencing practices through visual practice
- Marian Goodman, for growing a global eco-system of building capacity around presencing practices
- Dayna Cunningham, for teaching us how to bring presencing practices to

complex environments of systemic racism, and structural violence

- Ursula Versteegen, for bringing presencing practices into mindful agriculture
- Beth Jandernoa and the Circle of Seven for holding the space for all the above

  The u.lab core team
- Adam Yukelson, for co-creating the u.lab platform and leading the content creation of u.lab 1X ("From Personal Change to Prototype") and 2X ("Seven Acupuncture Points of Transforming Capitalism")
- Julie Arts, for facilitating the global u.lab Hub Host community and for leading the content creation of u.lab 3X ("How to create Your Innovation Lab: Pathway to Practice")
- Angela Baldini and Simoon Fransen, for facilitating and supporting the multi-local Hub Host and u.lab community
- Lili Xu and Jayce Lee, for inspiring and co-creating u.lab China and activating an amazing country-wide innovation eco-system around it

- Martin and Aggie Kalungu-Banda, for co-creating and prototyping u.lab Africa and working with numerous multi-stakeholder initiatives across the continent

Our core team partners in various parts of the world

- Frans Sugiarta, Dr. Ben Chan, and Shobi Lawalata, for co-facilitating and co-leading the u.lab and IDEAS programs in Indonesia in collaboration with United In Diversity
- Julia Kim and Ha Vinh Tho, for blending Gross National Happiness (GNH) with presencing practices in Bhutan, Vietnam, and Thailand
- Kenneth Hogg and Keira Oliver, for implementing u.lab in the Scottish government to activate ABCD (asset-based community development)
- Denise Chaer for pioneering the Food and Nutrition Lab in Brazil
- Katie Stubley, for building collective presencing capacity in Australia
- Manish Srivastava, for blending presencing practice and Gandhi inspired grassroots change in India
- Gene Toland, for creating a Latin American community of practice

- Reola Phelps and Wibo Koole, for the Sustainable Food Lab in Ethiopia
- Beth Mount, for blending inclusion work with Social Presencing Theater
- Liz Solms and Marie McCormick, for leading our L.A. Education Lab
- Dieter van den Broeck for applying the U process in ecosystem restoration
- Susan Skjei and Kathryn Schuyler for advancing awareness-based action research
- John Heller and our Synergos institute colleagues in lab initiatives around the world
- Cherie Nursalim and our United in Diversity colleagues from Indonesia and China
- Claudia Madrazo and our La Vaca Independiente colleagues in Mexico
- Wiebke König and Katharina Lobeck from GIZ Global Leadership Academy
  Our circle of advisers and board members
- Peter Senge, Ed Schein, Arthur Zajonc, Diana Chapman Walsh, Eileen Fisher, Isabel Guerrero, Becky Buell, Antoinette Klatzky, Christian von

Plessen, for co-inspiring PI from idea to global impact

And

- Janice Spadafore, for her magical skills in applying some structure to the dynamic chaos of all the above!

Much appreciation to my colleagues at MIT including Deborah Ancona and Phil Thompson, and to President Rafael Reif and Sanjay Sarma, MIT's VP for Digital Learning, for their leadership in creating MITx, edX, and spaces that allow platforms like u.lab to thrive.

Also a big thank you to Joseph Jaworski, Brian Arthur, John Milton, Eleanor Rosch, Ikujiro Nonaka, Francisco Varela, Nan Huai-Chin, Henri Bortoft, Betty Sue Flowers, Michael Jung, and Adam Kahane, who were critical contributors to the first articulation of Theory U through the book *Theory U* and the book *Presence* (co-authored with Senge, Jaworski, and Flowers).

Finally, I would like to thank Katrin for her significant input on the manuscript; Barbara Mackay, Jan Byars, and Rob Ricigliano for commenting on (parts of) the draft; Janet Mowery for applying her great editorial craft to the text; Kelvy for contributing the wonderful figures; Jeevan Sivasubramaniam for suggesting I write this book; and the entire Berrett-Koehler team for turning the manuscript into a book that I hope will be meaningful to you. Thank you all.

Enjoy the read!

*Otto Scharmer*
*Cambridge, MA*
*September 1, 2017*

# PART I

# A Framework for Seeing the Field

Some people say that, for all the talk about change, very little actually happens. But in my experience that is not true. I have seen tectonic shifts several times in my life. I saw it when the Berlin Wall collapsed in 1989—and with it the Cold War system. I saw it when the apartheid system ended in South Africa. I saw it when a youth movement swept the first African American president of the United States of America into office. I saw it when the center of the global economy shifted from the West to East Asia over the past two or three decades. And I see it now in the recent rise of autocrats, nationalists, and far-right movements as a counter-reaction to a single sided globalization and as an overlay to something of even higher significance: the awakening of a new awareness across the planet.

Even though not everyone of these changes amounted to a tectonic shift, this much I know: today, *anything can happen.* I believe that the most important tectonic shift of our lifetime is not behind but right in front of us. That shift has to do with **the transformation of capitalism, democracy, education, and self.**

1

# The Blind Spot

We live in a moment of profound possibility and disruption. A moment that is marked by the dying of an old mindset and logic of organizing. And one that is marked by the rise of a new awareness and way of activating generative social fields. What is dying and disintegrating is a world of Me First, bigger is better, and special interest group-driven decision making that has led us into a state of organized irresponsibility.

What is being born is less clear. It has to do with shifting our consciousness from **ego** -system to **eco**-system awareness—an awareness that attends to the well-being of all. In many places around the world we can actually witness the awakening of this awareness and its under lying force: an activation of the *intelligence of the heart.* Groups that begin to act from such an awareness can, in the words of UC Berkeley cognitive psychologist Eleanor Rosch, "be shockingly effective."

The beginnings of this shift may seem small and insignificant in comparison with the vast challenges that we face worldwide. And in many ways they are. Yet I believe that they hold the seeds for a profound *civilizational renewal* that is called for in order to protect and further activate the essence of our humanity.

FIGURE 1: The Challenge of Disruption

My friend and Presencing Institute co-founder Kelvy Bird captures this felt sense in the image of an abyss (figure 1).

If we picture ourselves on the left-hand side of the image, we can see a world that is disintegrating and dying (the structures of the past); on the right-hand side we see the new mental and social structures that are emerging now. The challenge is to figure out how to cross the abyss that divides the two: how to move from "here" to "there."

This picture, in a nutshell, depicts the journey of this book: the journey across the abyss, from a current reality that is driven by the past to an emerging future that is inspired by our highest future potential.

# Three Divides

Today this journey matters more than ever. If we look into the abyss, we see three major divides. They are:

- The *ecological divide:* unprecedented environmental destruction—resulting in the loss of nature.
- The *social divide:* obscene levels of inequity and fragmentation—resulting in the loss of society—the social whole.
- The *spiritual divide:* increasing levels of burnout and depression—resulting in the loss of meaning and the loss of Self. With the capital 'S' Self I

mean not the current ego self but the highest future potential.

The ecological divide can be summed up by a single number: 1.5. Currently our economy consumes the resources of 1.5 planets. We use 1.5 times the regeneration capacity of planet earth. And that is just the average. In the United States, for example, the current consumption rate has surpassed five planets.

The social divide can be summed up by another number: 8. Eight billionaires own as much as half of mankind combined. Yes, it is true. A small group of people that you can fit into a minivan owns more than the "bottom half" of the world's population: 3.8 billion people.

The spiritual divide can be summed up by the number 800,000. More than 800K people per year commit suicide—a number that is greater than the sum of people who are killed by war, murder, and natural disasters combined. Every forty seconds there is one suicide.

In essence, we are collectively creating results that (almost) nobody wants. These results include the loss of nature, the loss of society, and the loss of Self.

In the nineteenth century many countries saw the rise of the social divide as a major issue, and it has shaped our public awareness ever since. In the twentieth century we saw the rise of the ecological divide, particularly during the last third of the century. It too has shaped our public awareness.

And at the beginning of the twenty-first century we are seeing the rise of the spiritual divide. Fueled by the massive technological disruptions that we have experienced since the birth of the World Wide Web in the 1990s, advances in technology will replace about half of our jobs by 2050. We are now facing a future that "no longer needs us," to borrow the words of computer scientist and co-founder of Sun Microsystems Bill Joy, and that in turn forces us to redefine who we are as human beings and to decide what kind of future society we want to live in and create. After the various types of tyrannies that we saw throughout the twentieth century, are we now moving into a tyranny of technology? This is one of the questions we face when we look into the abyss.

In other words, we live in a time when our planet, our societal whole, and the essence of our humanity are under attack. That may sound a bit dramatic. Still, I believe it understates the significance of our current moment.

So where is the hope? The biggest source of hope in our time is that more and more people, particularly the younger population, realize that the three divides are not three separate problems. They are essentially three different faces of **one and the same** root issue. What issue is that? The blind spot.

# The Blind Spot

There is a blind spot in leadership, management, and social change. It is a blind spot that also applies to our everyday social experience. The blind spot concerns the inner place—the source—from which we operate when we act, communicate, perceive, or think. We can see *what* we do (results). We can see *how* we do it (process). But we usually are not aware of the *who:* the inner place or *source* from which we operate (figure 2).

Let me explain. I first stumbled onto this blind spot when talking to Bill O'Brien, the longtime CEO of Hanover Insurance. From his many years of leading transformational change, Bill summed up his greatest insight like this: ***"The success of an intervention depends on the interior condition of the intervener."***

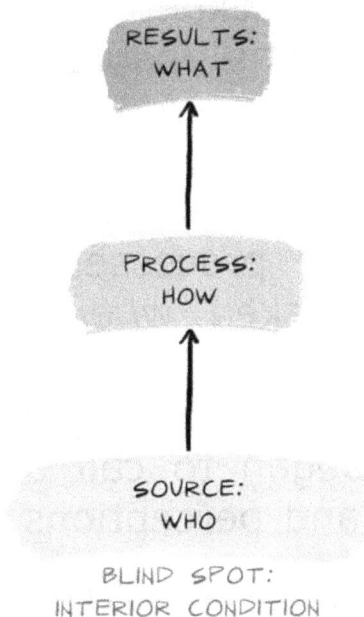

RESULTS:
WHAT

↑

PROCESS:
HOW

↑

SOURCE:
WHO

BLIND SPOT:
INTERIOR CONDITION

FIGURE 2: The Blind Spot of Leadership

Bill's statement opened my mind: What counts is not only what leaders do and how they do it but also their "interior condition"—that is, their inner *source.*

It dawned on me that Bill was pointing at a deeper dimension (the source) from which our actions, communication, and perceptions arise, and which allows us to sense and connect with a whole new set of future possibilities.

The quality of how we pay attention is a largely hidden dimension of our everyday social experience—whether it is in organizations, institutions, or even our personal lives. As we conduct our daily business, we usually are well aware of *what* we do and *how* we do it—that is, the processes we use. But if we were asked *where* our actions come from, most of us would be unable to provide a clear response. In my research I began to call this origin of our actions and perceptions the *source.*

# In Front of the Blank Canvas

Reflecting on my conversation with Bill O'Brien made me realize that, every day, we interact on both visible and invisible levels. To better understand this point, consider the work of an artist.

We can look at art from at least three perspectives:

- We can focus on the *thing* that results from the creative process—say, a painting.
- We can focus on the artist's *process* in creating the painting.
- Or we can observe the artist at the moment when she is standing in front of a *blank canvas.*

In other words, we can look at the work of art *after* it has been created, *during* its creation, or *before* creation begins.

If we apply this analogy to leading change, we can look at the change maker's work from three similar angles. First, we can look at *what* leaders and change makers do. Many books have been written from that point of view. Second, we can look at the *how,* the processes leaders use. We have used that perspective in management and leadership research for more than two decades.

Yet we have never systematically looked at the leader's work from the blank-canvas perspective. The question we have left unasked is: What *sources* are leaders and change makers actually operating from? For example: What quality of listening, what quality of attention, do I bring to a situation—and how does that quality change the course of action moment to moment?

To sum up the discussion of the three divides: While the ecological divide arises from a disconnect between *self* and *nature,* and the social divide arises from a disconnect between s*elf* and *other,* the spiritual divide arises from a disconnect between *self* and *Self*—that is, between who I am *today* and who I might be *tomorrow,* my highest future possibility.

# Arriving at MIT

When I arrived at MIT from Germany some twenty-four years ago, my goal was to learn how I could help change makers in society deal with the big challenges of disruption that keep coming our way. The then newly created MIT Organizational Learning Center (OLC), directed by Peter Senge, author of *The Fifth Discipline,* brought together a unique constellation of leading action researchers from MIT and Harvard, including Ed Schein, Chris Argyris, Don Schön, Bill Isaacs, and many others. This book is heavily shaped and inspired by the opportunity to work in this network and circle of wonderful colleagues and friends, along with many other valued collaborators from other institutions and places.

Looking back at my own journey today, I see three major insights and learnings that have shaped my journey of exploring the blind spot.

# Learning from the Future as It Emerges

My first insight is quite elemental. There are two different sources of learning: (1) learning by reflecting on the *past* and (2) learning by sensing and actualizing *emerging future* possibilities.

All traditional organizational learning methods operate with the same learning model: learning by reflecting on past experiences. But then I saw time and again that in real organizations most leaders face challenges that cannot be responded to just by reflecting on the past. Sometimes past experiences are not particularly helpful. Sometimes they are the very obstacles that keep a team from looking at a situation with fresh eyes.

In other words, learning from the past is necessary but not sufficient. All disruptive challenges require us to go further. They require us to slow down, stop, sense the bigger driving forces of change, let go of the past and let come the future that wants to emerge.

But what does it take to learn from the emerging future? When I started to ask this question, many people looked at me with a blank stare: "Learning from the future? What are you talking about?" Many told me it was a wrongheaded question.

Yet it was that very question that has organized my research journey for more than two decades. What sets us apart as human beings is that we can connect to the emerging future. That is who we are. We can break the patterns of the past and create new patterns at scale. No other species on earth can do this. Bees, for example, may be organized by a much higher collective intelligence. Yet they have no option to change their pattern of organizing. But we as humans do.

Let me say this in different words. We have the gift to engage with two very different qualities and streams of time. One of them is a quality of the present moment that is basically an extension of the past. The present moment is shaped by what has been. The second is a quality of the present moment that functions as a gateway to a field of future possibilities. The present moment is shaped by what is wanting to emerge. That quality of time, if connected to, operates from *presencing* the highest future potential. The word presencing blends "sensing" with "presence." It means to sense and actualize one's highest future potential. Whenever we deal with disruption, it is this second stream of time that matters most. Because without that connection we tend to end up as victims rather than co-shapers of disruption.

How can we connect to this second stream of time as individuals, as organizations, and as eco-systems? That exploration has guided my research journey over the past two decades. It has led me to describe a *deep learning cycle* that uses a different kind of process—one that moves us to the edges of the system, connects us to our deepest sources of knowing, and prompts us to explore the future by doing. This deep learning cycle applies both to our professional and our personal lives. For example, as a sixteen-year-old, I had an experience that gave me a real taste of what it looks and feels like to be pulled by the field of emerging future potential.

## Facing the Fire

When I left our farm house that morning for school, I had no idea it was the last time I would see my home, a large, 350-year-old farmhouse. It was just another ordinary day at school until about one o'clock, when the teacher called me out of class and said I should go home. I had no idea what might have happened, but felt it wasn't good news. After the usual one-hour train ride I ran to the entrance of the station and jumped into a cab. Long before the cab arrived, I saw huge gray and black clouds of smoke billowing into the air. My heart was pounding as the cab approached our long driveway. I recognized neighbors, area firefighters, and policemen. I jumped from the cab and ran through the crowd that had gathered, down the last half-mile of our chestnut-lined driveway. When I reached the courtyard, I could not believe my eyes. The world I had lived in all my life was gone. Up in smoke.

As the reality of the fire in front of me began to sink in, I felt as if somebody had ripped the ground from under my feet. The place of my birth, childhood, and youth was gone. As I stood there, taking in the heat of the fire and feeling time slow down, I realized how attached I had been to all the things destroyed by the fire. Everything I thought I was had dissolved. Everything? No, perhaps not everything, for I felt that a tiny element of myself still existed. *Somebody* was still there, watching all this. Who?

At that moment I realized there was another dimension of myself that I hadn't previously been aware of, a dimension that related to my future possibilities. At that moment, I felt drawn upward, above my physical body, and began watching the scene from that elevated place. I felt my mind quieting and expanding in a moment of unparalleled clarity. I was not the person I had thought I was. My real self was not attached to all the material possessions smoldering inside the ruins. I suddenly knew that I, my true Self, was still alive! It was this "I" that was the Seer. And this Seer was more alive, more awake, more acutely present than the "I" that I had known before. No longer weighed down by the material possessions the fire had just consumed, with everything gone, I was lighter and free, released to encounter the other part of myself, the part that drew me into the future—into *my* future—into a world waiting for me to bring it into reality.

The next day my eighty-seven-year-old grandfather arrived for what would be his last visit to the farm. He had lived in that house all his life, beginning in 1890. Because of medical treatments, he had been away the week before the fire, and when he arrived at the courtyard the day after the fire, he summoned his last energy, got out of the car, and went straight to where my father was working on the cleanup. Without seeming to notice the small fires still burning around the property, he went up to my father, took his hand, and said, "Kopf hoch, mein Junge, blick nach vorn!" ("Keep your head up, my boy, look forward!") Then, after a few more words, he turned, walked back to the waiting car, and left. A few days later he died quietly.

That my grandfather, in the last week of his life, with much of what he had been cultivating all his life gone up in flames, was able to focus on the emerging future rather than reacting to the loss, made a big impression on me.

Only many years later, when I had started to work on learning from the emerging future rather than from the past, did I start doing my best work. But I realize now that it was seeded in that early experience.

# Building the Container

"I hate when people say 'there are two types of people...,'" my MIT mentor Ed Schein said to me one day. Then, with the hint of a smile, he continued: "But there really are two types of people: those who understand process and those who don't."

Ed is right. Understanding **process** means to understand the making of our social relationships. If you want to change a stakeholder relationship from, say, dysfunctional to helpful, you cannot just order people to do it. You have to intervene further upstream in the process of social reality creation. You have to change the *making* of that relationship from one mode to another—for example, from reactive to co-creative.

Similarly, with respect to the "source" level of creativity, we can say that there are two types of people:

those who understand containers and those who do not. Container building is facilitator-language for forming a good holding space. Often in organizations you see CEOs and executives who fail to get that. They think they can create behavioral change just by making speeches and pushing tools onto the organization. Tools are important. But they are also overrated because they are so visible. But what is usually underrated is all the stuff that is invisible to the eye—for example, the less visible elements of a good holding space: intention, attention, and the subtle qualities of deep listening. Building a good container means to build a good holding space for a *generative social process.*

Much of the conventional language and toolkits around managing change turn out to be partially useful at best. For example, consider the term "driving change." When have you asked your family how much they like you to "drive" their web of relationships from one state to another? Good luck with that. The reality of leading profound change has little to do with one person "driving" the change of another. It is the wrong metaphor, the wrong approach. What I feel may be more useful is the metaphor of the farmer.

Which brings me to my third learning, and also back to my roots....

# Social Fields

I grew up on an 800-year-old farm near Hamburg. Sixty years ago, my parents decided to abandon conventional industrial farming techniques (using pesticides, herbicides, and chemical fertilizers) and replace them with organic methods (focusing instead on cultivating the living eco-system of the farm). Every Sunday my parents took me, my sister, and my two brothers on a *Feldgang*—a field walk—across the fields on our farm. Once in a while my father would stop, bend over, and pick up a clump of soil from a furrow so that we could learn to recognize its different types and structures. The quality of the soil, he explained, depended on a whole host of living entities—millions of organisms living in every cubic centimeter of the soil—whose work is necessary for the earth to breathe and to evolve as a living organism.

Just as we did on those field walks of my youth, this book will take you on a similar journey where every now and then we stop and examine a case story or a piece of data that helps us understand the deeper structures of the "social field." And just as the organic farmer depends completely on the living quality of the soil, social pioneers depend on the living quality of the social field. I define *social field* as the quality of relationships that give rise to patterns of thinking, conversing, and organizing, which in turn produce practical results.

And just as the farmer cannot "drive" a plant to grow faster, a leader or change maker in an organization or a community cannot force practical results. Instead, attention must be focused on improving the quality of the soil. What is the quality of the social soil? It is the quality of relationships among individuals, teams, and institutions that give rise to collective behavior and practical results.

Looking back, I realize that my journey over the past four decades has been one of cultivating social fields. My parents cultivated the fields on the farm. My colleagues and I cultivate social fields. And if you happen to be a manager, educator, entrepreneur, social entrepreneur, performing artist, health professional, parent, or movement builder, that is probably your work, too.

The deeper experiences and levels of the social field, described here, are familiar to everyone who is engaged in creating movements, startups or profound change. In my own case, I first got involved with the environmental, green, antinuclear, and peace movements of the late 1970s and 1980s, and later in launching the Presencing Institute as a new type of global social enterprise. Later in the book I will share some of those experiences in more detail. At this point I just want to draw your attention to the fact that none of these experiences are unique or extraordinary.

On the contrary, they are actually quite ordinary. Many people have them.

And yes, they do take you "out of the box," like the fire experience took me out of my physical body for a moment or two. And yet many of us have these experiences a lot more often than we realize at first sight.

# 2

# Theory U—Form Follows Consciousness

Theory U focuses on how individuals, groups, and organizations can sense and actualize their highest future potential.

You are probably familiar with the philosopher René Descartes's famous statement, "I think, therefore I am." That's not where we start from the Theory U vantage point. From a U perspective we would say, *I attend* (this way); *therefore it emerges* (that way). For example: the quality of my listening co-shapes how the conversation unfolds. Or, speaking more generally, the quality of results in any social system is a function of the *consciousness* from which the people in that system operate. Boiled down to three words, the idea can be expressed as **form follows consciousness.**

# Making the System See Itself

Over the past couple of decades I must have seen this happen hundreds of times: groups, sometimes large, sometimes small, going through a subtle shift in awareness in how they see, sense, and relate to each other, to their system, and to themselves.

Figure 3 depicts the mindset shift at issue here: switching from seeing the system as something "out there" (figure 3a) to seeing the system from a perspective that includes one's own self (figure 3b).

When that shift happens on an individual level, we call it *mindfulness.* Mindfulness is the capacity to attend to the experience of the present moment while *paying attention to your attention.*

When the same shift happens in a group, we call it *dialogue.* Dialogue is not people talking to each other. Dialogue is *the capacity of a system to see itself.* To see its own patterns. To see its own assumptions.

That capacity is, of course, also the essence of *systems thinking:* making the system see itself. Or, as we would say in the context of Theory U – based systems change: **making a system *sense and see* itself.**

When you deal with managing change then you know that the bulk of the job is moving people from a "silo view" to a systems view—or, as we would say, from an *ego*-system awareness to an *eco* system awareness.

In fact, what surprises me most is how reliably we can create conditions that allow for that kind of shift in awareness to happen. You can't manufacture it. You can't mold it like a piece of metal by hammering on it from the outside. But you can create a set of inner and outer conditions that allows a group, an organization, or a system to make that move, to sense and see themselves from the emerging whole.

Many people have asked me: How actually did you come up with the U framework? What are its origins? In this chapter, I will share mini-stories and ideas that illuminate the origins of Theory U. All interviews quoted can be found on the Presencing Institute website in the section Dialogue on Leadership (www.presencing.org).

FIGURE 3a: Seeing the System Out There
(Adapted from Andreas Gradert)

FIGURE 3b: Bending the Beam of Observation to Seeing System and Self (Adapted from Andreas Gradert)

# A Moment of Seeing

Shortly after I arrived at MIT in 1994, I watched a live broadcast on organizational learning facilitated by Peter Senge and Rick Ross, co-authors of the *Fifth Discipline Fieldbook.* In response to a question from the audience, Rick Ross went to the whiteboard and mapped the systems thinking "iceberg model" with the following words:

**Structure**
**Process**

# Mental Models

Seeing these words made me aware of two things. One is that organizational change happens on different levels. And two, probably there needed to be a fourth level beneath the three depicted on the whiteboard. When I wrote the three words down, I spontaneously added a fourth level that represented the *source.* Later I began to refer to the fourth level as "presencing."

Shortly thereafter I connected these four levels with the image of a U: One traveled down the left-hand side of the U from surface to source, differentiating levels of perception (projecting, perceiving, perceiving perception, intuition), and then up the righth- and side of the U, passing through different levels of action (envisioning, enacting, embodying).

Why did I use the U-shape? First, I was interested in depicting a *process* that showed the unearthing of the different system levels of the iceberg. Second, I had seen a different version of the U in two other places years before. One was in the work of the

Austrian organizational development and conflict resolution expert Friedrich Glasl. In his model he used the U to differentiate the levels of identity, people, and politics, and the techno-physical realm of organizations. The other place where I saw the U described as an evolutionary principle was in the work of the early twentieth-century educator and social innovator Rudolf Steiner. Reading Steiner was the key source of inspiration not only for me but also for Glasl. So, if any one person should be credited with originating the U process of evolutionary thinking, it should be Rudolf Steiner. A radical social innovator, Steiner has had a lasting impact; his institutional innovations include Waldorf schools, biodynamic farming, integrative medicine, phenomenological science, and a meditative path to self-development.

# The Process: Three Movements

Fast-forward four and a half years. Now we are in early 1999 and I am traveling with my good friend and colleague Joseph Jaworski, author of *Synchronicity: The Inner Path of Leadership,* to Xerox PARC in Palo Alto, California, a research site in the heart of Silicon Valley. It is a place that once housed what many even today consider the most creative team ever. That team created, among other things, laser printing, Ethernet, the modern personal computer, the graphical user interface, and other key features of what later became a multitrillion-dollar industry. Yet, ironically, its parent company, Xerox, never took full advantage of these inventions. But someone else did: Steve Jobs. The rise of Apple was basically a function of putting together all the key ideas that he saw at Xerox PARC. But back to our meeting.

We met with W. Brian Arthur, the founding head of the economics program at the Santa Fe Institute, who also had an office at PARC. Brian started by talking about the changing economic foundations of today's business world. "You know," he said, "the real power comes from recognizing patterns that are forming and fitting with them."

He went on to discuss two different levels of cognition. "Most tend to be the standard cognitive kind that you can work with in your conscious mind. But there is a deeper level. Instead of an understanding, I would call this deeper level a 'knowing.' Suppose that I was parachuted into some situation in Silicon Valley—not a real problem, just a complicated, dynamic situation that I'm trying to figure out. I would observe and observe and observe and then simply retreat. If I were lucky, I would be able to get in touch with some deep inner place and allow knowing to emerge."

He continued, "You wait and wait and let your experience well up into something appropriate. In a sense, there is no decision making. What to do becomes obvious. You can't rush it. Much of it depends on where you're coming from and who you are as a person. This has a lot of implications for management." Then he added, "I am basically saying that what counts is where you're coming from inside yourself."

What he said resonated deeply with what Bill O'Brien and many other innovators had shared with us earlier. Leaders need to deal with their blind spot and shift their attention to the inner place from which they operate. The conversation with Arthur furnished two principal insights. First, there is a distinction between two types of cognition: normal (downloading of mental frames) versus a deeper level of knowing. And second, to activate the deeper level of knowing, one has to go through a three-step process similar to Arthur's parachute example:

- Observe, observe, observe: connect to the places of most potential.
- Retreat and reflect: allow the inner knowing to emerge.
- Prototype: act from what emerges in the now.

On the flight back with Joseph, I drew a U figure on a piece of paper to visually map the three movements that Brian Arthur talked about (see figure 4).

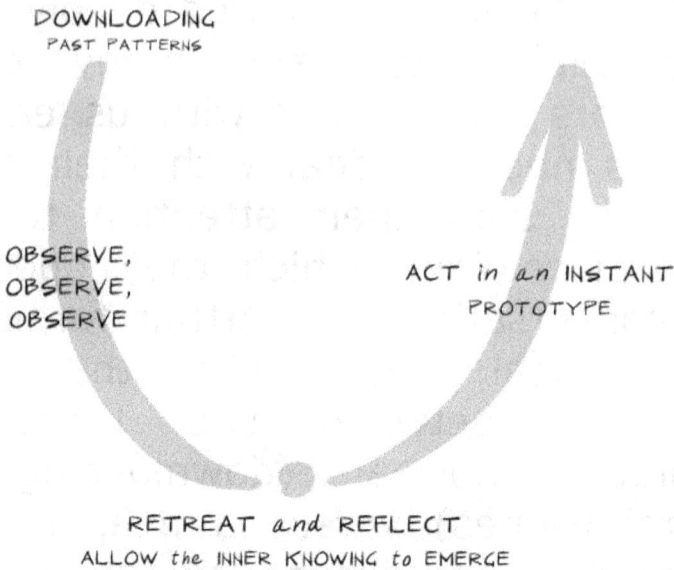

DOWNLOADING
PAST PATTERNS

OBSERVE,
OBSERVE,
OBSERVE

ACT in an INSTANT
PROTOTYPE

RETREAT and REFLECT
ALLOW the INNER KNOWING to EMERGE

FIGURE 4: The U Process—Three Movements

# Mapping the Deeper Territory

A few months later, in January 2000, I had the opportunity to meet with cognitive scientist Francisco Varela in Paris. Varela talked about the blind spot of cognition and brain research. "The problem is not that we don't know enough about the brain or about biology," he said. "The problem is that we don't know enough about experience.... We have had a blind spot in the West for that kind of methodical approach. **Everybody thinks they know about experience. I claim we don't.**"

Varela asked, "Can people cultivate the core process of becoming aware as an ability?" That core process, according to Varela, is composed of "three gestures of becoming aware: *suspension, redirection, and letting go.*"

We walked together through the three gestures. Varela explained. "By *suspension* I mean the suspension of habitual patterns. In Buddhist meditation, you put your butt on the cushion and move one level above your habitual engagement and see from a more aerial perspective." We went on to discuss how many people sitting in meditation claim that nothing happens. Why? "Because the whole point is that after suspension you have to tolerate that nothing is happening," he said. "Suspension is a very funny procedure. Staying with that is the key."

Then he explained the second and third gestures. *Redirection* is about redirecting your attention from the "exterior" to the "interior" by turning the attention toward the source of the mental process rather than the object. *Letting go* has to be done with a light touch, he cautioned.

Listening to Varela, I knew that I had seen these three gestures before. Like other facilitators, I have seen them many times in team processes with groups. Walking out of Varela's office, I saw in an instant how these gestures could be mapped onto the U. Figure 5 maps them on the left-hand side of the U, as gateways into the deeper layers of awareness; then, on the right-hand side, they are mirrored by their counter parts on the way up.

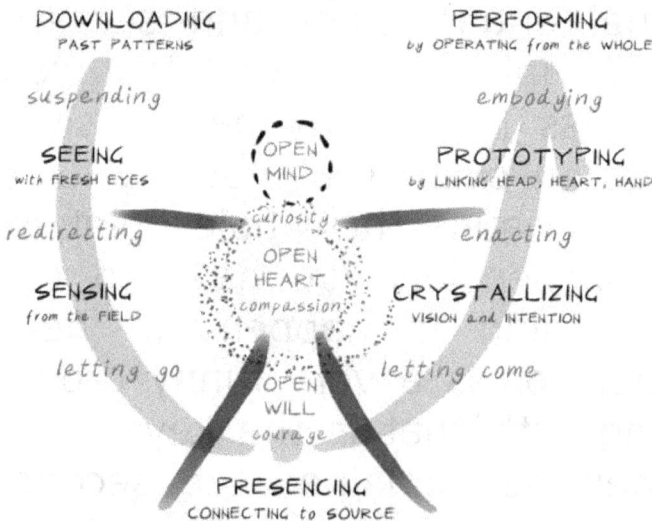

DOWNLOADING
PAST PATTERNS

PERFORMING
by OPERATING from the WHOLE

suspending

embodying

SEEING
with FRESH EYES

OPEN
MIND

PROTOTYPING
by LINKING HEAD, HEART, HAND

redirecting

curiosity

enacting

OPEN
HEART

SENSING
from the FIELD

compassion

CRYSTALLIZING
VISION and INTENTION

letting go

OPEN
WILL

letting come

courage

PRESENCING
CONNECTING to SOURCE

FIGURE 5: Theory U: Seven Ways of Attending and Co-shaping

The U integrates two different views of time: The shape of the U is a bow to the Eastern cyclical view, and the arrow is a nod to the Western linear view of development, which, as the ecological crisis demonstrates, is equally relevant. Figure 5 combines these views and shows **the core process of Theory U** and the seven ways of attending to and co-shaping the world. Whoever goes through this process experiences the following subtle shifts of the cognitive social field:

- **Downloading:** At the beginning there is a spark of becoming aware that moves us beyond downloading—beyond extending the patterns of the past. As long as we operate from downloading, the world is frozen by our old mental habits and past experiences; nothing new enters our minds. Same old, same old.

- **Seeing:** The moment we *suspend* our habitual judgment we wake up with fresh eyes. We notice what is new and see the world as a set of objects that are exterior to us, the observers.

- **Sensing:** The moment we *redirect* our attention from objects to source, our perception widens and deepens. This shift bends the beam of observation back onto the observer. The boundary between observer and observed opens up.
- **Presencing:** Entering a moment of stillness, we *let go* of the old and connect to the surrounding sphere of future potential. The boundary between observer and observed collapses into a space for the future to emerge.
- **Crystallizing:** As we *let come* and crystallize vision and intention, the relationship between observer and observed starts to invert. Envisioning happens from the field of the future (rather than from our ego).
- **Prototyping:** As we *enact* prototypes we explore the future by doing. The relationship between observer and observed continues its inversion. Enacting happens from "being in dialogue with the universe" (rather than from our ego).
- **Performing:** As we *embody* the new by evolving our practices and

infrastructures, the relationship between observer and observed completes its inversion. The embodying happens from the context of the larger eco-system (rather than from the small "s" institutional self).

In summary, the first key ideas of Theory U include the *three movements* that emerged from our conversation with Brian Arthur—observe, retreat (aka stillness), act—and the more granular *seven-point U* that emerged from my conversation with Francisco Varela. The third insight and key idea concerns the instruments of inner knowing.

# Three Instruments of Inner Knowing

The heart of Theory U concerns the interior dimension of the intervener that Bill O'Brien talked about. Today I would summarize this inner territory in terms of three instruments: open mind, open heart, and open will (figure 5).

An *open mind* is the capacity to suspend old habits of judgment—to see with fresh eyes. An *open heart* is the capacity to empathize and to look at a situation through the eyes of somebody else. An *open will* is the capacity to "let go" of the old and "let come" the new.

# The Example of Listening

Listening is probably the most underrated leadership skill. At the heart of most examples of colossal leadership failures—which are in no short supply—leaders are often unable to connect with and make sense of the "VUCA" world around them; that is, a world defined by volatility, uncertainty, complexity, and ambiguity.

Listening, however, is not only important to leadership. If you are not a good listener, there is no way that you can develop real mastery in any discipline.

The most consistent feedback we have received from the hundreds of workshops, programs, and innovation journeys we have facilitated is this: Shifting your mode of listening is life-changing. Shifting how you listen, the way you pay attention, sounds like a really small change. But here is the thing: Changing how you listen means that you change how you experience relationships and the world. And if you change that, you change, well, EVERYTHING.

And it is truly amazing how quickly people can shift their way of listening and attending. But it does take work: practice, review, peer feedback, and more practice. To become a better listener, you first need to understand the four archetypes of listening (see figure 6).

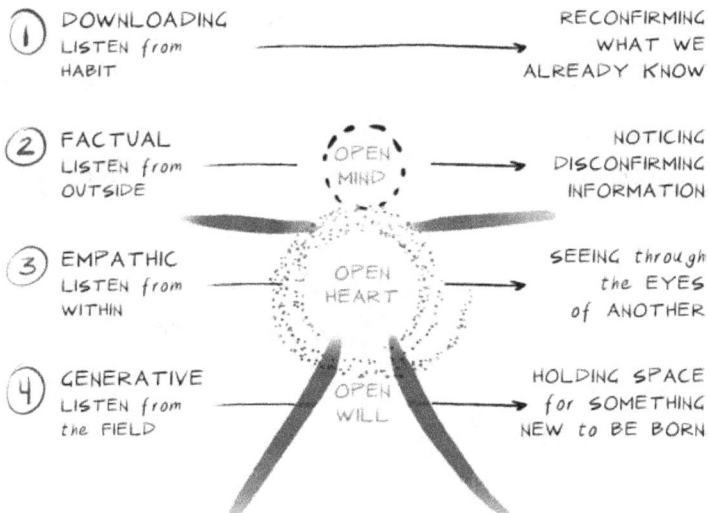

| | |
|---|---|
| ① DOWNLOADING LISTEN from HABIT | RECONFIRMING WHAT WE ALREADY KNOW |
| ② FACTUAL LISTEN from OUTSIDE | NOTICING DISCONFIRMING INFORMATION |
| ③ EMPATHIC LISTEN from WITHIN | SEEING through the EYES of ANOTHER |
| ④ GENERATIVE LISTEN from the FIELD | HOLDING SPACE for SOMETHING NEW to BE BORN |

OPEN MIND
OPEN HEART
OPEN WILL

FIGURE 6: Four Fields of Listening

The four types of listening reflect the under lying principles of the opening of the mind, heart, and will:

- **Downloading:** Listening is limited to reconfirming what we already know. Nothing new penetrates our bubble.
- **Factual listening:** We let the data talk to us and notice disconfirming information. Doing this requires opening the mind—that is, the capacity to suspend our habits of judgment.
- **Empathic listening:** We see the situation through the eyes of another. Doing this requires opening the heart: using our feelings and our heart as an organ of tuning in to another person's view.
- **Generative listening:** We listen for the highest future possibility to show up while holding a space for something new to be born.

When you listen on level 1, "downloading," your attention is not focused on what the other person says but on your own inner commentary. For example, you may be planning what you will say next. As you cross the threshold from downloading to factual listening (level 1 to 2), your attention moves from listening to your inner voice to actually listening to the person in front of you. You open up to what is being said.

When you start to cross the threshold from factual to empathic listening (level 2 to 3), your place of listening shifts from you to the other person—that is, from your small vehicle (the intelligence of your head) to your larger vehicle (the intelligence of your heart). You step into the other person's perspective. For example, you might think, "Oh, I may not agree, but I can see how she sees this situation."

Finally, when you cross the threshold from empathic to generative listening (level 3 to 4), your listening becomes a holding space for bringing something new into reality that wants to be born. You listen with openness to what is unknown and emerging.

What I have learned in my work is that the success of leadership and change work depends on the ability of the leader to observe his or her quality of listening and to adjust the quality of listening to what is needed in each situation.

# Three Enemies on the Journey Down the Left Side of the U

Why is the deeper territory of listening the road less traveled? Because it requires some intentional inner work to illuminate the blind spot, our interior condition. Connecting to our source of creativity at the bottom of the U requires crossing the three gates, or thresholds, as discussed. **What makes this journey so difficult is that these gates tend to be guarded by three "enemies"** (as I would say as an American) or **three "inner voices of resistance"** (as I would say as an European), each of which blocks the entrance to these deeper domains.

The first enemy blocks the gate to the open mind. Stanford University's Michael Ray calls this the *Voice of Judgment* (VoJ). Every creativity technique starts with this instruction: Suspend your voice of judgment. It is the critical starting point because without it we shut down the creative power of the open mind.

The second enemy blocks the gate to the open heart. Let us call this the *Voice of Cynicism* (VoC)—that is, all emotional acts of distancing. What is at stake when we begin to access the open heart? We must be willing to put ourselves in a position of true openness and vulnerability toward another, which is the opposite of distancing.

The third enemy blocks the gate to the open will. This is the *Voice of Fear* (VoF). It seeks to prevent us from letting go of what we have and who we are. It can show up as a fear of losing things. Or a fear of being ostracized. Or a fear of death. And yet dealing with that voice of fear is at the heart of leadership today: to hold the space for letting go of the old and for letting come, or welcoming, the new.

When you trace the Indo-European root of the word "leadership," you find *leith,* meaning "to go forth," "to cross the threshold," or "to die." Think about that: **The root of the word leadership means "to die."** Sometimes when you need to let go it feels exactly like that: dying. But what we have learned over the past two decades is this: A subtle inner threshold must be crossed before something new can show up, before the "field of the future" can begin to manifest.

# Two Barriers to Moving Up the U

Once you have crossed the threshold at the base of the U, there are two main challenges to moving up the right side of the U.

The first one is to **avoid mindless action.** Mindless action is when we blindly implement abstract ideas without any learning. The second challenge is the opposite of the first: to **avoid an action-less mind,** or "analysis paralysis." Analysis paralysis is maybe the biggest enemy of all prototyping: We discuss things to death instead of exploring the future by doing. So these are the two biggest challenges: avoiding an actionless mind and mindless action.

Thus the most important capacity on both sides of the U is to "stay with it." It is important neither to intervene too frequently by jumping in, nor to disengage by turning another way.

"Staying with it" means holding the space for something to be born that is not quite there yet—building and evolving the holding space for something new to develop and be born.

# Presencing and Absencing

Finally, the seventh idea of Theory U concerns the interplay of presencing and absencing. We know that there is a fair amount of *presencing* in the world: the sensing and actualizing of our highest future potential. Most of us have experienced it at special moments. Many of us know networks, communities, and places where this kind of operating happens fairly often. But most of us would be quick to acknowledge that our current age is also characterized by an enormous intensification of *absencing,* which is the opposite of presencing. Figure 7 maps the three "enemies" discussed previously, but in a slightly modified way, as:

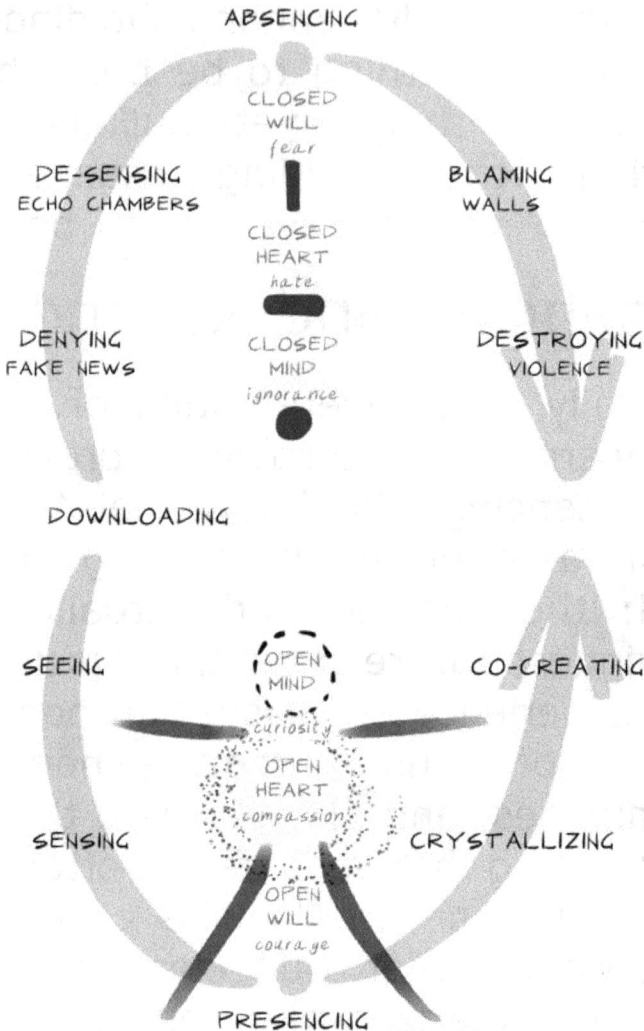

FIGURE 7: Two Social Fields, Two Cycles:
Absencing and Presencing

- Ignorance: the closing of the mind (stuck in One Truth)
- Hate: the closing of the heart (stuck in One Us vs. Them)

- Fear: the closing of the will (stuck in One Will)

What happens to a social system that operates on these principles? It creates an *architecture of separation* by building walls. It facilitates a disconnect (denying, de-sensing) from the world around us, from the world that is emerging (absencing), which results in blaming others (an inability to reflect) and destruction (of trust, relationships, nature, and self). This **cycle of absencing** is depicted in the upper half of figure 7.

The **cycle of presencing,** depicted in the lower half of figure 7, is based on:

- Curiosity: the opening of the mind
- Compassion: the opening of the heart
- Courage: the opening of the will

Social systems that operate on these principles enact *architectures of connection* that tear down the walls of separation.

## Social Fields

The cycle of absencing and the cycle of presencing denote different social fields. The cycle of absencing represents a field of destruction and social coldness. The cycle of presencing represents a field of co-creation and social warmth. Each field tends to be self-reinforcing. For example, once you are inside a cycle of absencing, inside a social dynamic of destruction, it is very hard to escape it.

Yet most people today, and most organizations and larger systems, experience being torn between these two fields. The field of presencing is experienced in many breakthrough teams, communities, and compassion-based social movements. Yet the field of absencing is likewise a central feature of our time. In fact, the entire space of public conversation, of media and social media, functions as a gigantic multiplier of absencing, but not of presencing. The use of Facebook for fake news and dark posts that helped Donald Trump by stirring up anger, fear, hate, and racism during the 2016 U.S. election cycle—funded by the Russian government and by U.S. billionaires—is a good example of the toxic impact of social media if technology is not used with an ethically sound intention (it was widely reported by BuzzFeed and others that people shared more fake news stories on Facebook than they shared stories from real news sites).

The question of course is: How can we create a mechanism that amplifies the cycle of presencing and the social field of curiosity, compassion, and courage? How can we design and create technology and social media for good? In the closing two chapters of this book we will come back to these questions. There I share an exciting joint initiative between HuffPost and the Presencing Institute that we are launching in 2018.

# 3

# The Matrix of Social Evolution

One of my most important insights is that there is a blind spot in learning and leadership. This blind spot concerns the sources from which our action and perception originate. **The aim of the Theory U method is to orient our attention to these *sources* of action and thought.** Our patterns of thinking, conversing, and organizing create a global world of social complexity that we enact moment to moment. How can we investigate the process of creating social reality? How can we catch the process of social reality creation in flight?

# The Grammar of Social Fields

In physics we learn that a material alters its behavior when it changes from one state to another. Water, for instance, at temperatures below freezing (32°F/0°C) forms ice. If we add heat and the temperature rises above 32°F/0°C, ice melts and becomes liquid water. If we continue to add heat and the temperature exceeds 212°F/100°C, water begins to vaporize into steam. In all three states the water molecules ($H_2O$) are the same, yet the material behaves very differently. This is also true for other materials: The molecules are the same, but the behavior can change.

In social fields, we see something comparable. When a group or a system shifts from one pattern of collective behavior (say, absencing) to another (say, presencing), the individuals in the system are still the same, but the connections among them are fundamentally changed, and that means that both the group and its members are no longer the same.

How can such patterns of interaction change from one state to another? If Bill O'Brien is correct that the success of an intervention depends on the interior condition of the intervener, then **leadership is the capacity *to shift*** *the inner place from which we operate.* In doing that, we shift the state of the social field. How exactly does that happen?

# The Matrix of Social Evolution

The first answer is that we start by learning to *see* the pattern language of social reality creation that we collectively enact. That is the focus of this chapter. The U is more than just a process. It is a nonlinear field theory that works as a matrix or a field.

*Social fields* describe the social system that we collectively enact—for example, the team, the group, the organization, or social system—**from the perspective of source.** The term "social field" illuminates the interiority of social systems and describes these systems both from the outside (the third-person view) and from within (the first-person view). It investigates the *interior conditions* under which social systems shift from one state of interaction to another.

Over many years working with groups and organizations, I have identified **four archetypes or qualities of social fields** that exist on all levels of systems: from micro to mundo. They are summarized in the matrix of social evolution (figure 8).

Take a moment to contemplate figure 8, which depicts the essence of this chapter in a nutshell. This map outlines a landscape of forms and qualities of social systems, which allows us to orient ourselves.

## *The Horizontal Axis: System Levels*

The four columns of the matrix feature the actions of individuals, groups, organizations, and systems. Social fields are enacted on all these levels through four primary forms of action: attending (micro), conversing (meso), organizing (macro), and coordinating (mundo). It is through these four activities that we as humans collectively create the reality we live in. Or, in the words of the late twentieth-century avant-garde artist

Joseph Beuys, these actions are how we create and live the global **"social sculpture."**

# The Vertical Axis: Levels of Consciousness

The vertical axis describes different states or qualities of our social reality. Remember the four types of listening? I can download old habits; I can open up and listen to facts; etc. The vertical axis summarizes these qualities of listening by differentiating four field states of awareness: habitual, ego-system, empathic, and generative. Each state of awareness has certain characteristic patterns or fields. They are:

**Field 1: Habitual.** When individuals, groups, or organizations operate with habitual field awareness, they interpret present situations based on their experiences and habits of the past.

**Field 2: Ego-system.** When individuals or groups start to suspend past assumptions and seek to see things "as they are," they enter a subject-object awareness in which they clearly differentiate between observer and observed. They begin to notice something new.

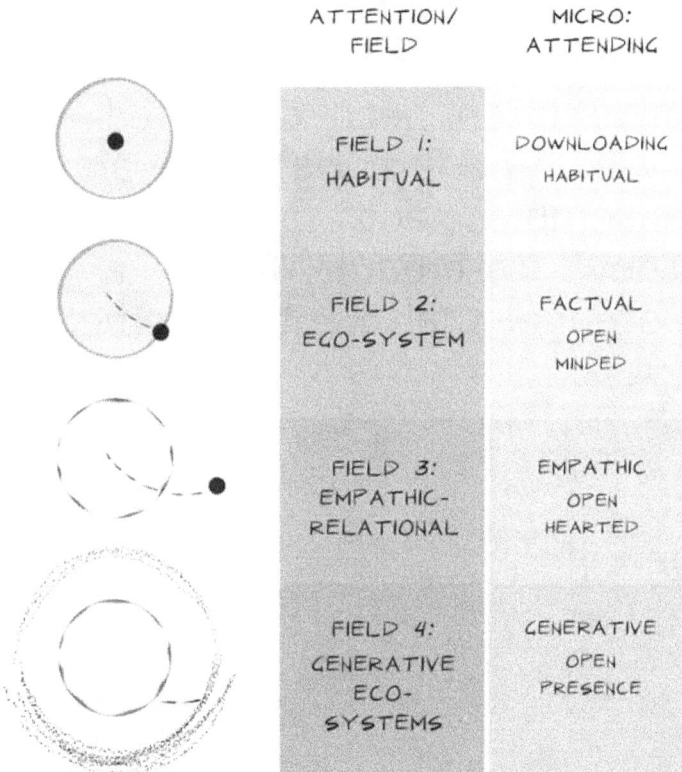

FIGURE 8: Matrix of Social Evolution

## Field 3: Empathic-Relational.

When actors in a system redirect their attention from object to sources and engage in an empathic awareness, they sense reality from the viewpoint of other stakeholders.

They begin to see from a new perspective.

**Field 4: Generative Eco-system.** When actors let go of old identities, a new space of co-creative awareness opens up. Actions from such shared awareness have often been described as *flow* by high-performing dance and music ensembles and by sports teams. They co-create from a future potential that wants to emerge.

| MESO:<br>CONVERSING | MACRO:<br>ORGANIZING | MUNDO:<br>COORDINATING |
|---|---|---|
| DOWNLOADING<br>TALKING<br>NICE | CENTRALIZED<br>TOP-DOWN | 1.0<br>HIERARCHY |
| DEBATE<br>TALKING TOUGH | DECENTRALIZED<br>DIVISIONS | 2.0<br>COMPETITION |
| DIALOGUE<br>INQUIRY | NETWORKED<br>STAKEHOLDERS | 3.0<br>STAKEHOLDER<br>DIALOGUES |
| COLLECTIVE<br>CREATIVITY<br>FLOW | ECO-SYSTEM<br>CO-CREATING | 4.0<br>ABC<br>AWARENESS-BASED<br>COLLECTIVE ACTION |

Now, take a look at the small icons in figure 9, where the location of the *source* is depicted as a dot that moves from the inside out (relative to the circle that represents the boundary of the system). These icons illustrate the four structures of attention, or the four different ways in which action and attention enter the world:

**Field 1: Habitual.** My action comes from inside my own boundaries (I-in-me). My reaction is triggered by external events and shaped by my habits of the past.

**Field 2: Ego-system.** My action comes from the periphery of my system (I-in-it). It arises from a subject-object awareness that analyzes and responds to exterior data.

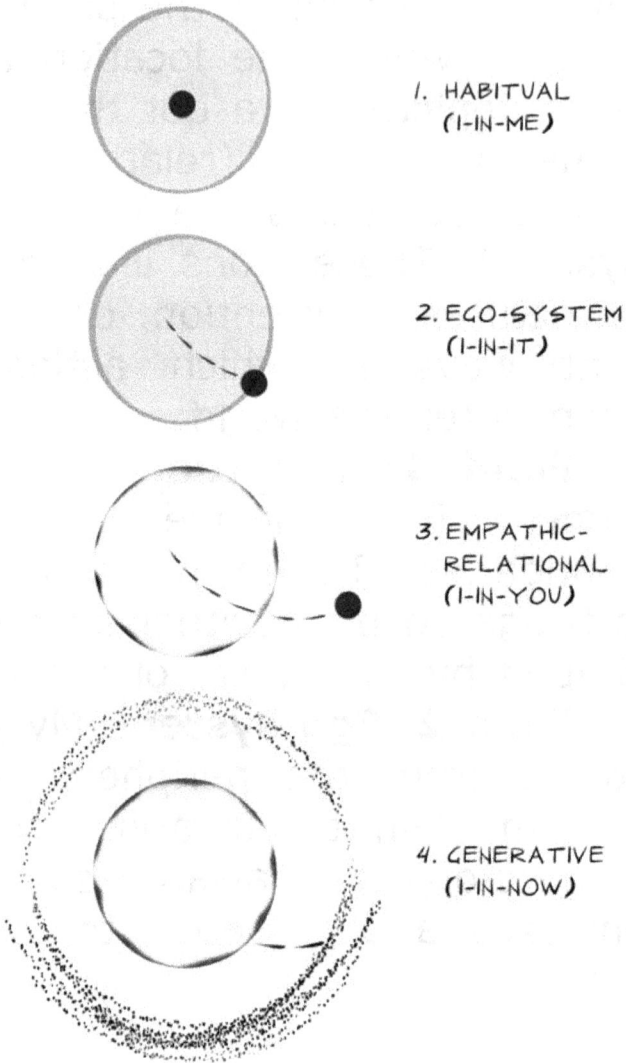

1. HABITUAL
(I-IN-ME)

2. EGO-SYSTEM
(I-IN-IT)

3. EMPATHIC-
RELATIONAL
(I-IN-YOU)

4. GENERATIVE
(I-IN-NOW)

FIGURE 9: Four Structures of Attention

## Field 3: Empathic-Relational.

My action comes from beyond my boundaries (I-in-you). It arises from the place that the other person, with whom I communicate, operates from.

**Field 4: Generative Eco-system.** My action comes from the sphere that surrounds my open boundaries (I-in-us/I-in-now). It arises from presencing a future potential.

**Every social action emerges from one of these four sources or structures of attention:** from *inside,* from the *periphery,* from *outside,* or from the *surrounding sphere* of a system. When we look at the social reality around us, most of the time we see that individuals, groups, and organizations operate from the first two states or stages. But great leaders, inspiring performers, disruptive innovators, and high-performing teams tend to operate from the *entire spectrum* of social fields, moving across all four of them *as needed* by the situation they face.

Just as we can see the work of a painter from different perspectives, we can view social action from the viewpoint of the completed picture (levels 1 and 2), from the viewpoint of the process (level 3), or from the viewpoint of the blank canvas or source (level 4).

# In Search of the Source

Here is a story that illustrates the fourth state of attention: I-in-now. One day several years ago I was hiking in the Alps, in Val Fex, a small valley near the border between Switzerland and Italy, right next to Sils Maria, where the philosopher Friedrich Nietzsche used to write. This area is a special place in Europe because it is the watershed for three major rivers: the Rhine, flowing to the northwest; the Inn, flowing to the northeast; and the Po, flowing to the south. I decided to follow the Inn to its source. As I hiked upstream, I realized that I had never in my life followed a stream all the way to its source. In fact, I had never seen what the source of a major river really looks like.

The stream grew narrower and narrower until it was not much more than a trickle. Soon I was standing near a small pond in the wide bowl of a valley, encircled by glacier-covered mountaintops. I stood there and listened and realized, with surprise, that I was at the center of countless waterfalls streaming off the mountains around me. They were making the most beautiful symphony of sound that one can imagine. There was no single point of origin. The source was surrounding me, streaming off the circle of mountaintops and then converging in an eco-system of small ponds. Was the pond next to me the source? Or was it in the symphonic sphere of waterfalls all around me? It is this kind of surrounding sphere that the fourth structure of attention (figure 9) embodies and depicts.

# Attending

The way I pay attention shapes how the social reality around me unfolds. ***I attend* [this way],** ***therefore it emerges* [that way].** Why? Because **energy follows attention.** Wherever you put your attention as a leader, as an innovator, as a change maker, or as a parent, that is where the energy of the system around you will go—including your own energy.

If the principle of *energy follows attention* is true, we need to cultivate and focus our attention. We all live in a culture where technologies and multitasking inhibit our capacity to sustain focused attention. The biggest enemy of our capacity to sustain attention is of course in our own pockets—the smartphones that help us in one moment and distract us in another. Research shows that a smartphone on your desk drains your brainpower even if it is turned face down and you do not even look at it.

Energy follows attention means that the key to great leadership and breakthrough innovation lies in our capacity for sustained attention. But that is not all. From a Theory U perspective, we focus not only on the *what*—what we pay attention to, but even more so on the *source:* the place from which our attention *originates.*

Earlier I introduced four different types of listening, each of which operates from a different source (figure 6):

- From my past experiences: habitual listening
- From my open mind: factual listening
- From my open heart: empathic listening
- From my open will: generative listening

If the essence of leadership lies in our ability to shift the inner place from which we operate, then this means that we need to develop the collective capacity to operate from all four types of listening, as required by the circumstances.

How do we develop this capacity? By practicing. Practicing every day.

**Downloading.** Whenever you sit in a meeting in which everything that happens confirms what you expected, then you are downloading. Downloading is neither good nor bad. It may be appropriate in one situation but not in another. It is just one type of listening. But if it is the only way you know how to listen, and if you happen to operate in an environment of disruptive change, then you are likely headed for trouble.

**Factual Listening.** Moving from downloading to factual listening is quite doable: Just pay attention to what is most surprising, most unexpected, or most interesting. Cultivate your curiosity and pay attention to everything that deviates from your earlier expectations (i.e., to disconfirming data). Capture these observations, for example, in a journal to make sure you do not lose them.

**Empathic Listening.** Moving from factual to empathic listening requires you to step into the perspective of another person. Taking this step requires you to love the other person to activate the intelligence of the heart. Sometimes that might not be easy. In such cases, you can begin by finding something that truly interests you about the other person, something that sparks your appreciation. "Switching on" your heart in this way helps you activate your source of empathic listening.

**Generative Listening.** Moving from empathic to generative listening is the most challenging. It is something that you cannot force. You can create conditions for generative listening. The most important intervention at this level is this: Do nothing. Do not intervene.

Do not disengage. Just stay with and hold the space for what wants to emerge.

I have often felt that listening is to a conversation what a welding flame is to a piece of metal. When you apply it briefly to a situation or to an object, what happens? Nothing. But if you keep that flame directed at a piece of metal, after a while the metal changes states from solid to fluid; suddenly you can mold the metal into different shapes. The same happens in conversations: as you continue to apply deep listening, over time the conversation will drop to a deeper level, to a different state.

# Conversing

Listening is an example of how people attend to the social reality around them. But going back to the landscape of the matrix: What is the action on the next system level? Conversation. **Conversation creates the world** we deal with in groups, organizations, and society.

1.  Conversations happen in fields—that is, conversations in groups tend to

follow certain patterns, and those patterns rarely change.

2. There is a limited set of conversational field patterns, meaning there is a limited set of qualities that a conversation can create in a social setting. The four different stages or qualities of conversation that I have observed, as shown in figure 10, are: **downloading** (field 1), **debate** (field 2), **dialogue** (field 3), and **collective creativity** or **presencing** (field 4).

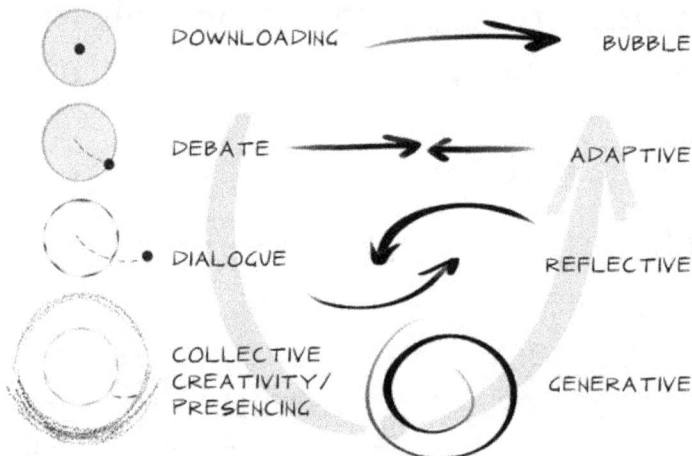

FIGURE 10: Four Fields of Conversation

The art of leadership is to facilitate shifts from one stage of conversation to another, depending on what is needed in a specific context and situation.

## Downloading: Enacting Conversations from Field 1

"How are you?" "I am fine."

Many formal meetings in organizations are conducted using this kind of ritualistic language. Operating effectively in such conversations requires that participants conform to the dominant pattern of exchanging polite phrases rather than saying what is really on their minds. In school, we learn to say what the teacher wants to hear. Later, we use the same skill to deal with bosses and to get ahead in organizations. If it serves us as individuals, what is wrong with it?

The problem is that this type of conversation—viewed from an organizational learning point of view—tends to result in completely dysfunctional behavior: It prevents teams from talking about what is really going on. They talk about the real stuff somewhere else—in the parking lot, on their way home. But in the workplace and in meetings, everyone's time is wasted when they do nothing more than exchange polite comments.

Downloading conversations simply reproduces existing phrases. Just as during individual downloading my perception of the world is limited to my existing mental frames and templates, conversational downloading articulates only those aspects of reality (as experienced by the participants) that fit into the dominant frameworks and conversational patterns of the group. The bigger the gap between what is said ("I am fine") and the actual situation ("I am about to die"), the higher the likelihood of some kind of disruption or breakdown in the system down the road.

# Debate: Enacting Conversations from Field 2

"How are you?" "I am terrible."

The defining feature of field 2 conversations is that participants speak their minds. For example, once, some twenty years ago, an audience member told me that he did not understand a single word of my presentation. Another example: An employee tells his CEO that some of his business practices are harmful and out of touch. These kinds of comments raise tensions. Everyone feels uncomfortable. This kind of conversation abandons rule-reproducing language for a tougher type of conversation in which individuals dare to differ.

The ticket to enter a field 1 conversation is the (unspoken) requirement to **conform.** The entry ticket to a field 2 conversation is the willingness to take a **different** stance. To get some airtime in a field 1 conversation you must conform to others' views (usually the boss's). In field 2, you suggest a different point of view. Just as in individual perception, the shift from downloading to seeing means being open to disconfirming data. Field 2 conversations imply opening up to viewpoints that challenge the dominant views.

The structure that results from this kind of interaction is often a debate. The word "debate" literally means "to fight or beat down." People use their arguments to beat or best their opponent, defined as anyone with a different opinion.

Debate and the expression of differing views can be useful in organizations because they put all the opinions on the table. In many Asian cultures, the best way to get participants into field 2 is by engaging people in small groups and allowing everyone to share their observations and views on a topic. The process is more like brainstorming different views than debating, which helps with issues of face-saving when confronting one's boss. Still, it delivers much of the same fundamental field 2 bottom line: the expression of diverse views.

But if an issue requires team members to reflect on and change their habits of thought and guiding assumptions, a different type of conversation than debate is needed—one that allows participants to realize that "I am not my point of view," as my colleague Bill Isaacs, author of *Dialogue: The Art of Thinking Together,* likes to say. I can suspend my own point of view and look at somebody else's assumptions. But to do so, I need to move into field 3.

## Dialogue: Enacting Conversations from Field 3

"How are you?"

"Not sure. But how are you, my friend?"

"Not sure either. I too arrived with an uneasy feeling."

"Oh, really? How interesting. Tell me about it. What's going on?"

Dialogue comes from the Greek *logos,* "word" or "meaning," and *dia,* "through," and can be literally translated as "meaning moving through."

Moving from debate (field 2) to dialogue (field 3) involves a profound shift in the collective field structure of attention through which a conversation operates. Just as the move from seeing to sensing on the individual level involves a shift from facing the world as an exterior set of objects to experiencing the world from the field, the shift from debate to dialogue also involves a shift from trying to beat down the contrary view to inquiring into each other's views, empathically listening from the other.

When this shift toward a dialogic field of conversation happens, your perspective widens to include yourself—you move from seeing the world as an exterior set of objects to seeing the world and yourself **from the whole.**

# Collective Presence: Enacting Conversations from Field 4

Level 4 generative conversations give birth to new ideas, imaginings, identities, and inspired energy. Examples include high-performing sports teams, jazz ensembles, and other groups in which musicians listen to themselves while simultaneously listening to the emerging collective music. When the quality of the listening and conversation moves into a generative stage, there are distinct changes in people's experience.

In field 4 conversations, the "How are you?" example reaches its limit. The shift into this deeper field of collective presence often happens in a transitional moment of stillness. That is why groups that want to access this deepest level often use intentional stillness as a gateway. It is a space of "doing nothing"—of neither over-intervening nor disengaging.

When that deeper generative field is activated, we usually experience it as *time* slowing down, *space* opening, widening, the sense of *self decentering,* while the *self-other* boundary opens up to a collective presence from which the conversation seems to flow. What I often experience in a generative dialogue is that ideas emerge collectively. People no longer say "This is my idea." Instead, the group engages in the art of thinking together where one idea builds on the other. The impact of this type of conversation can be profound, shaping or reshaping the course of one's life.

These shifts are well known by many experienced practitioners, innovators, top athletes, and great performers. Bill Russell, the legendary basketball player, wrote about these special moments in his 1979 book *Second Wind: The Memoirs of an Opinionated Man* (Random House, 155–158):

Every so often a Celtics game would heat up so that it became more than a physical or even mental game, and would be magical. That feeling is difficult to describe, and I certainly never talked about it when I was playing. When it happened, I could feel my play rise to a new level. It came rarely, and would last anywhere from five minutes to a whole quarter, or more.... It would surround not only me and the other Celtics, but also the players on the other team, and even the referees.

At that special level, all sorts of odd things happened: The game would be in the white heat of competition, and yet somehow I wouldn't feel competitive, which is a miracle in itself.... The game would move so quickly that every fake, cut, and pass would be surprising, and yet nothing could surprise me. It was almost as if we were playing in slow motion. During those spells, I could almost sense how the next play would develop and where the next shot would be taken.... My premonitions would be consistently correct, and I always felt then that I not only knew all the Celtics by heart, but also all the opposing players, and that they all knew me.

There have been many times in my career when I felt moved or joyful, but these were the moments when I had chills pulsing up and down my spine.

# Organizing

Global organizations are a new species on the face of our planet—a species that in less than two centuries has progressed to rule the world. Organizations are essentially geometries of power. They structure our collective decision making. When we look at the evolution of organizations, we see four different stages: centralized, decentralized, networked, and eco-system, which reflect different stages or qualities of how organizations operate. Again, the art is to develop tools that allow the organization to change and evolve into these different stages, depending on what is needed.

# Centralized

In 1.0 organizational structures, decision-making power is located at the top of the pyramid. It is centralized, top-down, often with formalized roles. These 1.0 structures work well as long as the guy (or core group) at the top is really good and the organization is relatively small and agile. However, once organizations or companies begin to grow, they need to decentralize in order to move decision making closer to the markets, customers, or citizens. The resulting 2.0 structures are defined by both hierarchy and competition.

# Decentralized

In a 2.0 organizational structure, decentralization enables the source of power to move closer to the periphery. The result is a functionally, divisionally, or geographically differentiated structure in which decisions are made closer to the markets, consumers, communities, or citizens. The good thing about 2.0 structures is the entrepreneurial in dependence of all of its divisions or units, its accountability, and its focus on meritocracy. The bad thing is that no one is managing the interdependence, the white space between the units. Which brings us to 3.0 structures.

# *Networked*

In 3.0 organizational structures the source of power moves even farther from the center. It originates from beyond the traditional boundaries of the organization. The result is a flattening of structures and the rise of networked relationships. Power emerges from the relationships to multiple stakeholders across boundaries. How many people report to me matters less than the quality of my stakeholder relationships inside and outside the organizations, or how many people follow me on Facebook and Twitter.

A good thing about 3.0 structures is empowerment and networked stakeholder connections. A bad thing is the increased vulnerability in the face of disruption or being sidetracked by vested interests, because small groups can organize their lobbying activities much more easily than large groups.

## *Eco-system*

Finally, 4.0 structures, or eco-system structures, operate by connecting and cultivating the entire living eco-system that is organized around a shared purpose. "Swarm" organizations and Agile or Teal-based organizations are all based on self-organizing circle structures in the context of shared purpose and institutional interdependency. As the decision making is being pushed even further to the frontline of organizations (empowering), these flattened and fluid structures of decision making only work well to the degree that the mindset of the participants has shifted from ego-system to eco-system awareness. This means that the decision-making circles develop the capacity to act from local knowledge while being aware of the cross-organizational interdependency and aligned by a shared purpose.

# Institutional Inversion

The evolution of today's organizational structures show a clear pattern: *institutional inversion,* that is, turning inside out and outside in. A simple example of inversion is this: Hold a sock in one hand and with the other reach deep inside it, pulling the toe back until you have turned it inside out. In the context of organizations, inversion applies to many of the core functions of management, as evidenced in the rise of crowdsourcing (inverted R&D), crowdfunding (inverted finance), swarm intelligence, and other ways of harnessing collective intelligence by inverting top-down silo-like structures to distributed organizing.

Thus, institutional inversion is a profound opening process that shifts the source of power from the top/center to the surrounding sphere. Let's look at an example.

# BALLE: Creating a Movement out of the White Dog Café

The Business Alliance for Local Living Economies (BALLE) has 22,000 members and is the fastest-growing network of socially and environmentally responsible businesses in North America.

The origins of BALLE lead us to the White Dog Café in Philadelphia and its founder and owner Judy Wicks, author of the memoir *Good Morning, Beautiful Business* (Chelsea Green, 2013). Over the course of twenty-five years, Judy has pioneered a series of groundbreaking business practices, including direct partnering relationships with local farmers and sustainable and local sourcing.

As she adopted these practices, the White Dog Café became more prosperous and successful. But instead of resting on that success, Judy decided to do something different. She realized that if she really cared about the well-being of her community and environment, she needed to help her competitors learn how to do what she was already doing.

In a 2011 interview conducted by Elizabeth Hoffecker Moreno of MIT—from my book *Leading from the Emerging Future: From Ego-system to Eco-system Economies*—Wicks said, "It was a transformational moment, when I realized that there is no such thing as one sustainable business, no matter how good the practices were within my company, no matter if I composted and recycled and bought from farmers and used [renewable] energy and so on, that it was a drop in the bucket. I had to go outside of my own company and start working in cooperation with others, and particularly with my competitors, to build a whole system based on those values."

To move into this environment, Judy established the White Dog Café Foundation in 2001, which she funded with a portion of the profits from her restaurant. The first project of the foundation was Fair Food (www.fairfood philly.org) whose original purpose was to provide free consulting to White Dog's competitors—the chefs and local restaurant owners in Philadelphia—to teach them how to buy humanely raised pork and other products from local family farms and why it was important.

Also under the umbrella of the foundation, in 2001 Judy cofounded BALLE to build a network of place-based businesses using practices that could grow into a viable alternative to the corporate, chain-store economy. Thus the story of Judy Wicks and The White Dog Café starts with a simple structure (centralized), later morphs into a more decentralized networked structure (helping competitors with the Foundation), and finally results in a purpose-driven eco-system of place-based business communities.

Today this evolutionary pattern is evident in most industries. When you look at sustainability efforts in the fashion industry, or "clean disruptions" in transportation and energy, you see challenges that require new patterns of industry-wide collaboration and learning.

# Coordinating and Governing

The fourth primary action (the mundo level in figure 8) concerns governance and connecting to social systems on the societal level. A dominant factor in shaping societies is our economic system. Distribution of labor has been the key to the amazing jumps in productivity of our modern economies. But it comes with a question: How do we coordinate the whole? In recent history, we have seen three different responses to that question—that is, three different coordination mechanisms—and today we see the rise of a fourth.

According to the British historian Arnold Toynbee, societal progress happens as an interplay between challenge and response: Structural change happens when a society's elite can no longer respond creatively to major social challenges; old social formations are therefore replaced by new ones. Applying Toynbee's framework to the coordination challenge of capitalism today, let us briefly review its evolution to date.

# Society 1.0: Coordinate around Hierarchy

Think of Europe at the end of the Thirty Years' War in 1648. Think of Russia after the October Revolution in 1917, China after the Chinese Civil War in 1949, or Indonesia at about the time Sukarno became its first president. Turmoil had created the felt need for stability—that is, for a strong visible hand, sometimes in the form of an iron fist—to provide security along with the vital allocation of scarce resources in line with much-needed public infrastructure investment. In that regard, we can view twentieth-century socialism in the Soviet Union not as (according to Marxist theory) a post-capitalist stage of economic development, but as a pre-capitalist (quasi-mercantilist) stage. The core characteristic of this stage of societal development is a strong central actor that holds the decision-making power of the whole.

# Society 2.0: Coordinate around Competition

The positive accomplishment of a state-driven society, primarily driven by field 1 structures, is its stability. The central power creates structure and order, with a calming of the chaos that preceded it. The downside of Society 1.0 is its lack of dynamism, and in most cases a lack of individual initiative and freedom.

Historically, the more successfully a society meets the stability challenge, the more likely this stage will be followed by a shift of focus from stability to growth and greater individual initiative and freedom. This shift gives rise to markets and a dynamic entrepreneurial sector that fuels economic growth.

At this juncture we see a whole set of institutional innovations, including the introduction of markets, property rights, and a banking system that provides access to capital. These changes facilitated the unprecedented explosion of economic growth and massive industrialization in nineteenth-century Europe and that we are seeing in China, India, Indonesia, and other emerging economies today.

Awareness during this 2.0 stage of development—primarily driven by field 2 structures in the terminology of figure 8—can be described as an awakening ego-system in which the self-interest of economic players acts as the animating force. The dark side of this stage includes negative externalities such as unbounded commodification and its unintended side effects, including child labor, human trafficking, environmental destruction, and shocking levels of poverty and inequality.

# Society 3.0: Coordinate around Interest Groups

The great accomplishment of the laissez-faire, free-market economy is growth and dynamism; the downside is that it has no means of dealing with the negative externalities that it generates. Measures to correct these problems include the introduction of labor rights, social security, environmental protection, and federal reserve banks that protect the national currency, all of which are designed to do the same thing—limit the unfettered market mechanism in areas where it does not work.

The regulations and changes in the institutional framework that resulted from this stage represent the efficacy of a third coordination mechanism: negotiation and dialogue among organized interest groups.

As societies evolve, sectors differentiate: first the public or governmental sector, then the private or entrepreneurial sector, and finally the civic or nongovernmental organization (NGO) sector. Each sector has its own set of enabling institutions. Stakeholder capitalism (Society 3.0) deals relatively well with the classical externalities through wealth re distribution, social security, regulation, subsidies, and the like. However, it fails to react to the global challenges of our time, including peak oil, climate change, resource scarcity, mass migration, and changing demographics. The limitations of 3.0 societies and their bias in favor of special interest groups, its reactive approach to negative externalities, and its limited capacity for intentionally creating positive externalities.

# Society 4.0: Coordinate around Common Awareness of the Whole

Twenty-first-century problems cannot be addressed with the twentieth-century vocabulary of problem solving. Each of the evolutionary stages described operates with a different state of awareness: Economies in 1.0 societies operate according to the primacy of traditional awareness; in 2.0 economies we see the awakening of self-interest or ego-system awareness.

In 3.0 economies, this self-interest is widened and mitigated by the self-interest of other stakeholders who organize collectively to bring their interests to the table through labor unions, government, nongovernmental organizations, and other entities.

In the emerging 4.0 stage of our economy, the natural self-interest of the players extends to a shared awareness of the whole eco-system. Eco-system awareness requires us to open the heart and to internalize the views and concerns of other stakeholders. The result is decisions and outcomes that benefit the whole system, not just my part of it.

For more detail on the 4.0 economy, see chapter 6 and the book *Leading from the Emerging Future: From Ego-system to Eco-system Economies* (Berrett-Koehler Publishers, 2013).

# Field 1 to Field 4: A Journey of Inversion

If we use Matrix of Social Evolution as depicted in figure 8 as a diagnostic tool, we can easily see the main problem with organizational and societal change today: That we are **trying to solve level 4 problems by responses and routines that are limited to levels 1–3**—ignoring Einstein's dictum that you cannot solve problems with the same level of thought that created them.

So how are we helping individuals, groups, organizations, and systems to advance their capacity to operate from across the entire matrix as needed, rather than being boxed into row 1 and row 2?

We will address and answer that question later in this book. For now let's just say that we started this chapter by talking about the state shifts from solid to fluid to vapor that happen when we apply heat to ice and then to water. When you read the columns of the matrix (figure 8) you see the various evolutionary states and stages of the social field. The biggest insight here is that **the shifts in awareness and consciousness along the vertical axis of the matrix are the same across all columns.** That was the big insight I had as I walked out of Francisco Varela's office.

Moving down the matrix from level 1 to level 4 takes us through a process of *opening* and *deepening.* "Opening" means to take what is inside our microcosm and make it part of the larger macrocosm around us: As we open the mind, the heart, and the will, we begin to connect with the intelligences that are surrounding us: **the Mind of the collective, the Heart of the collective,** and **the intention or Will of the emerging field.**

| FIELD | TIME | SPACE | OTHER |
|---|---|---|---|
| FIELD 1. HABITUAL | DISEMBODIED | 1-D | COMFORMING |
| FIELD 2. SUBJECT -OBJECT | CHRONOS | 2-D | CONFRONTING |
| FIELD 3. EMPATHIC- RELATIONAL | SLOWING DOWN | 3-D | CONNECTING |
| FIELD 4. GENERATIVE | STILLNESS/ KAIROS | 4-D | COLLECTIVE PRESENCE |

FIGURE 11: Matrix of Social Evolution: The First-Person View

"Deepening" means to internalize what is outside, to deepen our own interiority. The combined process of turning inside out and outside in is what I refer to as *inversion.*

To be an effective leader or change maker, we need to go through the same inversion: Open up to the intelligences that are surrounding us and deepen our own interiority.

What does such a generative field experience look like from a first-person perspective? The changes that my colleagues and I have experienced include the following (see also figure 11):

| SELF | MATERIALITY | AGENCY | THINKING |
|---|---|---|---|
| HABITUAL | ABSENT | RULE-REPEATING | FROM HABITUAL PATTERNS |
| RATIONAL | RESOURCE | RULE-REALIZING | FROM THE HEAD |
| RELATIONAL | LIVING SYSTEM | RULE-REFLECTING | FROM THE HEART |
| EMERGING HIGHER SELF | LIVING PRESENCE | RULE-GENERATING | FROM PRESENCING/ THE WHOLE |

- **Time slows down.** "It was almost as if we were playing in slow motion" while the boundary between the present and the emerging future collapses, as Bill Russell put it.

- **Space widens.** In moments of profound shifts in group processes, participants often sense a widening of the surrounding collective space, particularly upward.
- **The self-other boundary collapses.** Russell wrote about the collapse of the boundary between his team and their opponents: "It would surround not only me and the other Celtics, but also the players on the other team, and even the referees."
- **The self begins to "de-center."** This awareness is sometimes also referred to as panoramic awareness. Russell seems to refer to a panoramic awareness of the entire field, including "all the opposing players."
- **Materiality changes.** The quality of matter and sensual perception also shifts. For example, in moments when social presencing happens, workshop participants often report a "thickening" and "warm" quality of the light.

- **Agency changes:** from **rule-repeating** to **rule-generating** or "operating from the source." Operating from the source often comes with the experience of a presence that is not mecentered but operates *through* me.
- **Thinking changes:** from habitual thinking to thinking from source: **presencing.**

# Making the System Sense and See Itself

Anyone who lives in this century and who observes how we collectively enact our social fields could have filled in the boxes of the two tables (figures 8 and 11) on their own. Looking at these tables is like **looking into the mirror of our evolution** and seeing the patterns that we enact individually and collectively. It is a pattern language that, across the levels of the matrix, **bends the beam of observation back onto our evolving self.**

What are the driving forces of this evolutionary movement that sometimes seems to move backward (as we are seeing in the age of Trump)? There are two main driving forces. One works from *outside:* the challenges of disruption that force us to stop, let go, and let come. These are manifest in the ecological, social, spiritual, and digital disruptions that are happening as we speak.

The other driving force works from *within:* the spontaneous awakening of a new awareness, of a new sense of connection to each other, to the planet, and to our future possibilities. How to cross the threshold to our deeper sources of awareness is the focus of chapter 4.

# 4

# The Eye of the Needle

Often in my work with groups and organizations, I experience a moment that feels like approaching a threshold at the bottom of the U. If that threshold is not crossed, all the talk about change is hollow and disconnected. I sometimes call that threshold the eye of the needle. In ancient Jerusalem there was a gate called "the needle," which was so narrow that when a fully loaded camel approached it the camel driver had to take off all the bundles so that the camel could pass through. Referring to this well-known image of his day, Jesus said, "It is easier for a camel to go through the eye of a needle than for a rich man to enter the kingdom of God." Likewise, in order to cross the threshold at the base of the U, we must drop everything that is not essential.

I have seen this subtle shift in many presencing retreats. When people return from their solo experience in nature, be it after one day, two days, or just a half-day, you see and sense immediately a shift of tone. In the circle sharing that follows the solo, when participants reflect on their experiences, many of them speak about their life and work journey as if a new pair of eyes had opened for them. They see themselves from a higher vantage point, and they look at the journey as a whole instead of as a series of daily situations. They recognize their habitual patterns, their deeper intentions, what matters most to them, their aspirations for themselves and for their community. In short, nothing is the same.

Crossing that threshold means to be willing to let go. To let go of old patterns, assumptions, and even our old "ego-self." Only then it is possible to step into our dormant potential, our emerging "Self."

It is not as abstract as it may sound. It is subtle, as my friend and colleague Peter Senge likes to point out. Let me illustrate this with two stories in which something that happened changed my sense of who I am. This chapter explores the more personal side of the shift, and the remaining chapters explore the organizational and systemic side.

# "I Expect a Lot from You"

During my student days in Germany at Witten/Herdecke University, where I was studying economics and management, some of my fellow students and I were also reading the works of philosophers that we were interested in.

They included Plato, Aristotle, Nietzsche, and some contemporary philosophers. One of them was Vittorio Hösle; inspired by Hegel, he linked the ecological crisis of our time to the evolution of philosophical thought. Having read more than a thousand pages of his work, I finally dared to ask his office for a meeting (at the time, he was teaching at the University of Essen, not too far from my university).

He agreed. My heart was pounding when I entered his office. What was I thinking? How could I, an unknown student, ask for a meeting with someone who in my intellectual universe was on nearly the same level as Plato, Aristotle, or Lao Tzu. He was very friendly, answering every single one of my prepared questions. I was stunned that he would treat me almost as if I were a peer. I was amazed and almost in disbelief. Then, suddenly, our time was up.

As I packed up my recording devices, out of the blue he turned to me and said: "You know, I expect *A LOT* from you in the future!"

What? Who was he talking to? To me? Can't be. But there was no one else in the room. Time stopped. Maybe, it dawned on me, he was talking not to the person that *I* knew as me. Maybe he was talking to another part of me—one that he could see and that I could not. All of this happened in maybe five seconds—yet it felt like half an eternity. In that moment I had a strange feeling of being pulled slightly upward into a space of unknown possibility.

When I left Hösle's office, I was no longer the same person. I had met a philosopher, a teacher, who saw something in the student that planted a seed. It was a seed of awareness that made the student less certain, and maybe less rigid, and more open to future possibilities that had been beyond his own imagination. Fun fact: In 1999, Hösle moved from Germany to the United States and has been teaching since then at the University of Notre Dame. I have not had any direct interaction with him since that exchange some twenty-five years ago....

# Reintegration of Matter and Mind

Fast-forward another three years. Having moved to Cambridge, Massachusetts, I started a second round of interviews with innovators, sponsored by McKinsey and Company. One of them was with Peter Senge. Peter started by talking about a recent experience he had in Hong Kong. "I had an interesting conversation with Master Nan, the Chinese Zen master Nan Huai-Chin,"

Peter said. "In China he's a very revered figure. He's considered an extraordinary scholar because of his integration of Buddhism, Taoism, and Confucianism. I asked him, 'Do you think that the industrial age will create such environmental problems that we will destroy ourselves and that we must find a way to change industrial institutions?'

Master Nan paused and shook his head in response. Peter continued, "He didn't completely agree with that. It wasn't the way he saw it. He saw it at a deeper level, and he said, 'There's only one issue in the world. It's the reintegration of matter and mind.' That's exactly what he said, the **reintegration of matter and mind.**"

As I listened to Peter's story, those words struck a deep chord. I felt an essential question slowly taking shape in my mind: What does the split between matter and mind really mean in the context of society today? I was reminded of my parents' work on their farm. The visible result of farming, the harvest, depends on the quality of the soil. So I wondered: *What if the quality of the visible social-economic outcomes is a function of the invisible social soil that resides in the blind spot of our perception?*

# The Essence of Systems Thinking

I asked Senge how he saw the separation of mind and matter relating to our world of organizations. Organizations, he responded, work the way human beings create them. Yet people inside these organizations maintain that it is "the system" that causes their problems. It is always something external, some "thing" that imposes itself on them. So the reality might actually be: Thought creates organizations, and then organizations hold human beings prisoner, or, as quantum physicist David Bohm used to say, "Thought creates the world and then says 'I didn't do it!'"

"To me," continued Peter, "here's the essence of what systems thinking is about: People begin to consciously discover and account for how their own patterns of thought and interaction manifest on a large scale and create the very forces by which the organization then 'is doing it to me.' And then they complete that feedback loop. The most profound experiences I've ever seen in consulting have always been when people suddenly say things like, 'Holy cow! Look what we are doing to ourselves!' or 'Given the way we operate, no wonder we can't win!' And what is always significant to me, in those moments, is the **we.** Not 'you,' not 'them,' but 'we.' ... A true systems philosophy closes the feedback loop between the human being, their experience of reality, and their sense of participation in that whole cycle of awareness and enactment."

I had read a lot about systems thinking, but I had never thought about it this clearly and simply: **The *essence of systems thinking* is to help people close the feedback loop between the enactment of systems on a behavioral level and its source on the level of awareness and thought.**

To that comment, Senge responded quietly, "Yes, I don't think I've ever thought about it quite this way any time before."

I left that conversation as a different person. Something subtle had been reordered and shifted within myself. It felt as if I had somehow encountered an essential aspect of my own question. I couldn't fully verbalize the question, but I could feel it very strongly. It was physical—a distinct bodily sensation that lasted for a week or two. When it began to fade, I started to think about it in terms of seeing the deeper sources of social reality creation, the deeper conditions from which social action arises moment by moment. *What if the visible outcomes of the social field, the tangible actions, are a function of the social soil, of the interior conditions—that is, of the invisible part of the field?*

That question put me on a path toward discovering the principles of Theory U, including the matrix of social evolution (figure 8). What is the essence of the matrix? It is the **reintegration of matter and mind.** Field 1 is based on a complete separation of matter and mind—the downloading of an empty, hollow, lifeless body of phrases and routines: *rule-repeating* behavior. Field 4 is based on the complete reintegration of matter and mind, which creates *rule-generating* behavior that becomes a vehicle for the future to emerge.

# Through the Eye of the Needle

Both the "matter and mind" encounter and the "I expect a lot from you" story exemplify moments when something happens that shifts or clarifies your sense of who you really are and the future that you want to co-create.

My meeting with Vittorio Hösle strengthened my pursuit of a path that made me leave the well-worn trail. The mind-and-matter conversation with Peter Senge led me to Master Nan in Hong Kong and to many other visits to China, eventually anchoring my current work not only in the West, but also in East Asia.

To pass through the eye of the needle requires three conditions: the opening of our mind, heart, and will. Open Mind means no judgment, allowing the **Mind of the universe** to operate through your thinking. Open Heart means no cynicism, allowing the **Heart of the collective** to operate through your feelings. Open Will means no fear, allowing the **Intention of the emerging future** to operate through your actions.

No one has articulated this subtle shift at the bottom of the U better than Martin Buber, who wrote these words in *I and Thou* (1923):

He must sacrifice his puny, unfree will, that is controlled by things and instincts, to his grand will, which quits defined for destined being. Then, he intervenes no more, but at the same time he does not let things merely happen. *He listens to what is emerging from himself, to the course of being in the world; not in order to be supported by it, but in order to bring it to reality as it desires.* (italics added)

# Inverting the System-Self Relationship

The shift at the base of the U is not a singular event. It is an awareness and presence that is always accessible to us. The journey of the U is a journey to that deeper place and encounter. The more we can sustain this deepened connection, the more we find that our relationship to the "system," to the social field, is shifting. The seven following mini-stories illuminate how my self-system relationship has been transformed over the years. I am using my personal experience here because this is where I have access to "first-person data," the inner shifts and changes that occur in such a process.

## *The Battle of Brokdorf*

In this first story I reacted to a system that was completely outside of me. *The system was the enemy.*

In my youth, during the late 1970s and early 1980s, I became an activist in the Green movement in Germany. Back then, one of the main battlefields of that movement was Brokdorf, a small town in northern Germany that happened to be not too far from my home. Brokdorf was the construction site of an atomic power plant that today has already been shut down. One day my friends and I went to Brokdorf to protest the plant's construction, along with about 100,000 people from all over Germany. The march was not legal, and the site was guarded by a massive police force, but all was peaceful until the end, when we were about to head home and the police started to attack. Suddenly we heard a deep, rhythmic drumming and loud shouting. We turned to see hundreds, possibly thousands, of heavily armed police beating their batons on their battle shields and running toward us. Everybody knew what to do next: Run. The police chased us over the fields like chickens. As the distance between us and the police closed, I first heard and then saw a swarm of helicopters approaching. They flew so low that people to my right and left were pushed to the ground by the force of the wind from their propellers. Without stopping, I looked back to see what had happened to them. They were surrounded by baton-swinging cops.

Half an hour later, those of us who had escaped were walking quickly and quietly, tightly bunched together, on a broad highway back to our buses and cars. A deep-red setting sun bathed the whole scene in cinematic light. When the sun had almost set, just before we reached our vehicles, the police attacked again, erupting from the woods on our left with batons swinging. As they approached us, shouting, something strange happened: Everyone in our large crowed stopped and stood absolutely still, all of our bodies close together as if we were one big collective body. Nobody ran. Everything stopped in a moment of total stillness. Then in the next moment the police began beating the people within reach of their batons. Still the crowd did not react. Their truncheons cut into our collective body like knives through butter. After a short while they realized that no one was fighting back. The collective body remained still. Surprised by that, the police stopped and soon retreated.

When I returned home that night, I was a different person. I had seen the enemy. *That system* is the enemy (as the famous line in the movie *The Matrix* goes). I knew in my bones what I would do with the rest of my life.

## Moving Inside the System

Three years later, I was a university student in my freshman year. In this story my relationship to the system morphs from enemy to inquiry. I chose to study economics and management at Witten/Herdecke University. I wanted to understand and alter the core DNA of our economic order. After the first week or so every student had to choose a mentor company in which to spend a day a week and much of the summer break in order to "learn by doing." Given my background with the peace movement, I did not want to have anything to do with the military-industrial complex. So I picked a textile company in Wuppertal. I liked the CEO, Erich Colsman, for several reasons, including his use of art practices to build management capacities. Fun fact: A week into my first internship I came across a bunch of machines that were producing an olive-green cord. I asked what that was for. "Oh yeah," was the response, "those are parachute cords for the German air force." So much for my avoidance of all things military. My illusion that I can separate myself from the system only lasted a few weeks.

## Learning How to Be Helpful to Change Makers

The events in this third story changed my relationship between self and system by teaching me how to be helpful. In 1994 I had just applied to the MIT Learning Center. I did not know anyone there when they invited me to some interviews. My final conversation was with Bill Isaacs. He said: "Okay, we like what you do, but we have a hiring freeze here at MIT. Can you bring your own funding?"

"Of course I can," I heard myself responding before I could even think about it. Two months later I moved to MIT to continue my journey. Of course

I had no funding. Worse than that, I still had student loans to pay back. So, with a maxed-out credit card and no resources available from friends or family, I realized that I had to be innovative. I had to learn how to build helping relationships—aka "process consultation." In this area I found tremendous value in the work of my MIT mentor Ed Schein.

Fun fact: Back then I tended to silently complain to myself, "Why does everyone else get their research funded and I don't?" Little did I know that it was exactly that lack of funding that would force me to immerse myself in fascinating, hands-on innovation and experiments.

Thus my focus shifted toward working **inside** the system. I learned, somewhat to my surprise, that "the system" as such does not really exist. What does exist are coalitions of stakeholders that want to move the system one way, and other coalitions of people that want to move it another way. And many more in between. I learned how to see the cracks in the old system and how to use them as windows of opportunity for experimenting with systemic change.

## *A Moment of Clarity*

Fast-forward almost another decade, to September 2003. His Holiness the Dalai Lama held his first public dialogue with leading brain scientists of the Western world. The location: MIT's Kresge Auditorium, the biggest on campus. Our friend and colleague, the physicist Arthur Zajonc, was the host and moderator of the event. At the end of that meeting I was filled with energy and excitement about the power and possibilities of investigating a field that linked the worlds of science (the third-person view) and consciousness (the first-person view). During those two days I felt, though, that the conversation was entirely ignoring a third dimension that was necessary to frame the inquiry: the dimension of social transformation and change.

When I left the MIT auditorium, together with Katrin, Dayna, and Peter, I could see, in a flash, EVERYTHING that was WRONG with my life: I was going in too many different directions, pursuing far too many projects in too many places. As that message—You must change your life!—was sinking in, I saw in a flash what I should be focusing on instead. I should concentrate all my energy on a **single** project: To create a place—a "global action research university"—that integrates science, consciousness, and social change with practical, hands-on experiments that evolve the system.

In this story the boundary between system and self collapsed: There was no such distinction. There was just one very clear thing: a calling and a knowing in my bones that would reorient the rest of my life.

## Co-imagining: Activating the Mind of the Collective

What comes after such a moment of unparalleled peak clarity? An extended period of decline and a dissipation of clarity. There are always excuses for why it is impossible to do this or that. But in this case my period of decline did not last that long. The main reason for that was a circle of friends and colleagues in Cambridge, Massachusetts, that included Peter Senge, Arthur Zajonc, Diana Chapman Walsh, Katrin Kaufer, Jon Kabat-Zinn, Dayna Cunningham, and Arawana Hayashi. We alternated meeting between Katrin's and my place in Cambridge and Diana Chapman's place at Wellesley College, where she was serving as president at the time. The name of the circle was the S3 group—for the integration of science, spirituality, and social change.

For a number of years in the early 2000s we met every three or four months, discussing a wide range of topics but always focusing on reimagining the twentieth-century university that integrated the three S's. That shared imagination has occasionally materialized in collective action, including during Arthur Zajonc's tenure as president of the Mind and Life Institute, as well as in several related lines of work at the Presencing Institute and the Society for Organizational Learning (SoL).

In terms of the relationship between system and self, the S3 circle story differs from my earlier stories in one important respect: Instead of responding to an exterior system that is already there (as in my experience with police violence, the textile company, or client projects), this line of work started with my and our initiative to form a circle of individuals who **co-imagined** a new space of possibility. The primary reality was not the exterior system, but a shared imagination that resulted from jointly leaning into the emerging future.

## Co-inspiring: Activating the Heart of the Collective

Another two or three years went by. For a while I had been noticing that the client interventions I was doing, even though they were fun, almost always focused on issues inside these organizations. We never addressed systemic or societal issues that crossed institutional boundaries, which I had come to believe were most important.

So one day, supported by Katrin, Dayna, and Peter, I stopped complaining and finally started doing something. I began talking to CEOs and executives of major global players in business, NGOs, and government, including some multilaterals. "Look, we know that major disruptive challenges are coming our way, and we know that no organization can prepare their next generation of leaders to respond to these disruptions alone" was the kind of pitch that I brought to them. "Therefore, would you be willing to send two or three of your best high-potential leaders to spend part of their time in a multisector innovation lab learning to confront future disruptions and to co-create new ways of operating across their institutional boundaries?"

Somewhat to our surprise, almost everyone said yes. Long story short, we called this project ELIAS (Emerging Leaders Innovate Across Sectors) and wound up with a wonderful group and lab experience. The personal impact was life-changing for just about everyone in the ELIAS lab group of 28 participants. The short-term prototypes developed were promising, but the longer-term impact of these initiatives was stunning.

The prototypes focused on a range of issues, from zero-emission vehicles to renewable energy to using design thinking for policymaking. One group replicated the trisector ELIAS approach on a national level, first in Indonesia and later in various provinces in China.

Nothing I had ever done before came anywhere close to having the combined impact of this initiative. Yet no one had asked me to do it. It was born out of observing the system, noticing what happens and what does not occur, getting frustrated about the mismatch, and then noticing an intention emerging from that experience which finally led me to do something about it.

In hindsight, I believe that ELIAS activated a *generative social field* across individuals and institutions—it activated the intelligence of the heart, and with it an enormous level of trust that, among these individuals, will never fade. In this mini-story we, the faculty, focused on holding the space. We didn't tell the participants what to do. We just gave them the process and the tools, and we helped them to co-inspire a generative social field. But then they took over.

## Co-creating: Activating the Will of the Collective

In 2013 I was meeting at MIT's Management School with Katrin, Dayna, and Phil Thompson, all three from the Department for Urban Studies and Planning (DUSP). Phil had just shared his impressions from a DUSP faculty meeting with President Rafael Reif in which Reif gave an inspiring speech about reinventing education and learning at MIT. When he finished, the four of us looked at each other and knew it was clear that we would have a lot to offer in terms of new formats, methods, and tools. But how to line up with such an institutional innovation opportunity was a big question. I felt frustration creeping up from within. A feeling well known by everyone who feels as a misfit, coming from the bottom, and trying to change the paradigm of a system. But then the four of us had a really creative conversation about what might be possible.

The next morning I sent an email to President Reif. A few hours later he had connected me with Sanjay Sarma, the head of Digital Learning. Sanjay suggested that I turn my MIT u.lab class into a MOOC—a massive open online course. Both he and Reif have been pioneers for turning MIT into a global leader in the massive democratization of knowledge by making all educational content available for free and to all. Their initiative has created what today is one of the top two global online learning platforms: edx.org. I happily agreed to Sanjay's proposal.

Ten months later, in 2015, we launched the first u.lab MOOC. Today, in 2017, we have had over 100,000 registered participants from 186 countries. Thus within about one year the size of my class went from 50 on campus to 50,000 through the u.lab MOOC.

How did that happen? How do you reinvent your own role as an educator in a radically decentralized classroom? We will talk about that more later. At this point, let us just say that my role in teaching a class at MIT and my role in co-facilitating this global eco-system with hundreds of local communities are different, primarily because in the latter the classroom is so decentralized and self-organized.

We ended the first u.lab cycle by saying, "Thank you so much—it has been such a wonderful experience co-creating this experience with you. This session completes our program." And here is what we heard back from the participants: "What are you talking about? You can't end this thing here! Haven't you noticed what's happening? Something is being born. A community of inspired change makers who collaborate for a better world."

So, reflecting on this feedback in our u.lab core team with Adam, Kelvy, Julie, Angela and Lili, we added another session to the calendar and went on a listening journey to the u.lab hubs in many locations in order to learn from them what worked, what did not work, and what to aim for next on our collective journey.

In this story of co-creation our attention again focuses on holding the space for a global community to be born—and to evolve.

# From Reacting to Regenerating

I tell these mini-stories to demonstrate how my relationship between system and self has morphed and transformed over the years. It started with the system as the enemy. Then it evolved from seeing my connection to the system, to seeing the cracks, to learning how to help change the system. The later stories of coimagining, co-inspiring, and co-creating are all variants of the same type operating through what Martin Buber so eloquently talked about: "He listens to what is emerging from himself, to the course of being in the world; not in order to be supported by it, but in order to bring it to reality as it desires."

That type of attention focuses on both the inner and the outer; on holding the space for something that is wanting to be born to manifest. The slight difference among these three examples concerns the degree to which the future is co-defined. In the first example the future is largely co-defined (co-imagining), while the future in the second example is less (co-inspiring), and in the third example is least defined (co-creating).

By presenting these stories in a linear order, I did not want to claim a too linear progression here. In reality its more complex, more multi-layered, more back and forth. But I do want to draw your attention to this subtle source dimension that is often ignored: **that the key leverage point for transformational change starts with attending to how you as a change maker relate to the system** that you want to change and to the system that you want to give birth to.

# PART II

# A Method for Consciousness-Based Systems Change

I believe that the number-one leadership challenge in the world of business, government, and civil society is the same. It is to enable stakeholder groups that need each other to change the system to move from **me** to **we**—that is, from *ego* -system awareness to *eco* system awareness.

How do you do that? Chapter 5 shares a method, a path that has evolved from countless experiments and applications over the past two decades.

5

# One Process, Five Movements: Innovating from the Future

Presencing is an innovation method that enables groups and stakeholders to co-sense and co-create the future. Profound innovation requires us to suspend downloading patterns in order to activate generative social fields. The five movements of the U process are:

Co-initiating: uncovering shared intention—building a first container

Co-sensing: seeing reality from the edges of the system—establishing the horizontal connection

Co-presencing: connecting to your highest future potential—establishing the vertical connection

Co-creating: prototyping to learn by doing—bringing the new into reality

Co-shaping: embodying and institutionalizing the new—evolving the larger eco-system

Here is a quick overview of the key principles and practices of this process.

# Co-initiating: Uncovering Shared Intention

The starting point of the process is to build a container for a core group that is going through the process together. This first stage lays the foundation for the later process and its impact. This first step of co-initiating focuses on uncovering common intention. Listening is the key:

- Listening to your own intention or to what life calls you to do (listening to oneself)
- Listening to your core partners in the field (listening to others)
- Listening to what you are called to do now (listening to what emerges)

*Company example:* When I worked with a medium-size "green" bank that uses finance to address social and ecological challenges, the executive board decided the bank needed to reinvent its business model. The CEO invited a core group that included members of the executive team, some country directors, and others who were viewed as critical for developing a new strategic perspective as well as translating opportunities into prototypes.

During a two-day kickoff meeting the group identified the forces driving disruption in their industry and ranked them according to relevance. They asked: What small changes can have a big impact on the system we operate in? What variables can affect the evolution of our industry? One factor the team identified was "sustainability goes mainstream." The group knew that 83 percent of GenY populations want to see business take a stance on issues such as sustainability. So the bank's challenge was to figure out how a green and socially conscious bank can differentiate itself in a market when its former key differentiator has become mainstream.

Another driving force was digital disruption. The old business model is challenged by fintechs (tech ventures that offer financial services) that disrupt traditional services by delivering services better, cheaper, and faster. As Bill Gates put it: "Banking is necessary, banks are not." After identifying and prioritizing these driving forces, the group created a blueprint for planning the co-sensing learning journeys (overviewed in the next section). The group also generated an initial intention statement and questions that would guide the lab journey.

*Multi-stakeholder example:* Novos Urbanos Social Innovation Lab on Food and Nutrition in Brazil was the idea of one person, Denise Chaer, a young social entrepreneur from São Paulo. While attending the Foundation program of the Presencing Institute in São Paulo, she dreamed up the idea to change consumption behaviors and social-economic relations in major cities in Brazil. In a series of dialogues and focus groups, she homed in on one important element of the system: food and nutrition.

Denise invited a microcosm of the system that she wanted to change, representatives of the food and nutrition system, into the room. She included experts and activists but also consumers and others affected by the existing system. This diverse group then began to map the system as a whole, which allowed each of them to see their specific contribution to the problem, whether it was the large multinationals selling sugary drinks in schools, or parents not encouraging healthy eating habits at home. The map that this group developed is still used by experts in Brazil to describe the food system and its challenges.

# Outcomes of Co-initiating

Whatever you do during the movement of co-initiation, make sure that by the end of that stage you have established the following:
1. A shared intention of what you want to create
2. Critical questions you need to explore

3. A core group that guides the initiative
4. A core team to dive into the U process
5. Deep listening and conversation practices
6. An effective support structure
7. Resources: people, place, bud get
8. An initial set of driving forces to explore
9. An initial list of possible learning journeys
10. An initial roadmap for the way forward

## Principles

The method of the U is summarized in 24 principles that are presented in five groups along the moments of the U from co-initiating to co-shaping. I will number them throughout the movements to indicate that the 24 principles work as a whole. Here are the first five:

**1. Listen to What Life Calls You to Do**
The essence of the U process is to strengthen our ability to be present and consciously co-create. Just as Ed

Schein's approach to process consultation (PC) starts with the principles "Always try to be helpful" and "Always deal with reality," the U process of presencing starts with the primacy of attention and intention: "Listen to what life calls you to do." Or, in the words of Martin Buber: "[She] listens to what is emerging from [herself], to the course of being in the world; not in order to be supported by it, but in order to bring it to reality as it desires." The U method is firmly grounded in process consultation as one of its principal parent disciplines.

## 2. Listen and Dialogue with Interesting Players on the Edges

The second domain of listening takes you out of your familiar world and to the edges and corners of the system. Connect and talk to interesting players in the larger eco-system of your relationships. Talk to both the visible core players and the less visible ones—including people from marginalized and underserved communities that do not have a voice in the current system. As you proceed on your mini-journey, let yourself be guided by the field. Focus on emerging opportunities. The most important helpers, partners, and guides often turn out to be different from what you expect; therefore your inner work is to stay open to suggestions.

## 3. Clarify Intention and Core Questions

Do not rush the first step of clarifying the intention and core questions that guide the inquiry. When working with designers from the consulting company IDEO, I have been impressed by how much time they spend up front, before beginning a project. "The quality of the creative design process," one IDEO leader explained, "is a function of the quality of the problem statement that defines your starting point."

## 4. Convene a Diverse Core Group around a Shared Intention

Convene a constellation of players that need one another to take action and to move forward. The opposite of co-initiation is marketing—getting people to "buy in" to your idea. That almost never works because it is just your idea. So part of the art of convening these players is to loosen your own grip on the idea—without necessarily giving it up. You lead by painting a picture that is intentionally incomplete; you make a few strokes and you leave lots of blank space so that others can make a contribution. In this way you shift the power dynamics from individual to shared owner ship, and from owner ship to belonging, to seeing your part in a larger social field. The quality of the impact of your initiative depends on the quality of the shared intention by the core team.

## 5. Build the Container

And the quality of that shared intention largely depends on the quality of the container, the holding space that shapes and cultivates the web of relationships. The most important leverage point for building a high-impact container is right at the beginning, when you **set the tone,** when you evoke and activate the field. Container building includes outer and inner conditions, the most important of which is collective listening to the different voices and to the whole. The example of the Circle of Seven, which is told in the section on Presencing below, provides more detail on this aspect of the work.

# Practices

Here are a few core practices that I rely on in my role as convener or facilitator, particularly during the co-initiation stage of the work.

## Practice 1

Start the day with an intentional silence. Intentional silence or mindfulness allows you to let go of the noise and everything that is not essential, and to connect with the purpose and intention that you want to be in service of. That attunement sets the tone for the day.

## Practice 2

End each day with four or so minutes of observation, as if you are looking at yourself from outside. Pay attention to how you interacted with others and what other people wanted you to do. Do this nonjudgmentally.

Just observe. Over time, you will develop an internal observer that allows you to look at yourself from someone else's point of view.

## Practice 3

To activate your generative listening, you have to fall in love with the person you are listening to. Sometimes that is not so easy. In those cases, switch on your abundant appreciation for and loving interest in the other person (or some aspect of her) within yourself. This is an inner attitude that we can intentionally activate. If you are unable to do this, then at least begin by creating a welcoming place for that other person in your heart.

## Practice 4

When you co-initiate with potential partners, always remember to:
- Clarify your intention to serve the evolution of the whole.
- Trust your "heart's intelligence" when connecting with people.
- Be open to other ways of framing the problem or opportunity (different stakeholders emphasize different variables).

- Connect to potential partners through their highest future sense of purpose, not just their institutional role or responsibility.
- When convening a core group, consider including key players and "crazy" activists—that is, people who would give life and soul to make it work—as well as people with no voice in the current system.
- Create a hospitable place.

## *Born in the Blizzard*

In December 2005, Katrin and I invited a small group of practitioners, researchers, and activists to begin co-initiating a platform for a global presencing-in-action school. About a dozen of us met in Cambridge, Massachusetts, in early December. We decided to walk the short distance from MIT to the SoL offices on the Charles River, a walk that usually does not take longer than ten minutes. But that day it was snowing, and as we walked the snow piled up and the visibility grew worse. No cars passed us. It was as if we were lone actors in a Siberian slow-motion movie. The blizzard offered us a special form of walking meditation. Later that day, as the storm intensified, we heard thunder and saw lightning strike nearby. That was the first time any of us had experienced that rare combination: a blizzard along with lightning and thunder. We took it as Mother Nature's way of welcoming us. In that first co-initiation meeting, we aspired to create a holding space for awareness-based change, for cultivating the conditions for profound civilizational renewal. The meeting was personal, aspirational, but did not result in anything even close to a grand (or not so grand) plan. But it set a tone and intention.

# Co-sensing: Seeing Reality from the Edges of the System

Having initiated a common intention with a core group, the next step is to form a team to take a deep-dive innovation journey through the stages of co-sensing, presencing, prototyping, and institutionalizing. The *core group* (which often includes executive sponsors) and the *team* (the people that make it happen) tend to overlap. In small systems the overlap could be 100 percent. But in most complex systems it is less.

The essence of co-sensing is getting out of one's own bubble. Our virtual bubbles (social media echo chambers), our institutional bubbles (organizational echo chambers), and our own affinity bubbles (the kind of people we like to hang out with) keep us in the world of downloading: same old, same old. At its core, cosensing is about immersing yourself in new contexts that matter to your situation and that are unfamiliar to you.

Why does it matter? Cognitive scientist Francisco Varela shared with me this story about an experiment with kittens. It takes newborn kittens a couple of days to open their eyes. In this experiment, newborn kittens were bundled in pairs of two, one on the back of the other. In each pair, only the lower kitten was able to move. The upper kitten (the one on the other's back) experienced the same spatial movements—but without performing the legwork, which was left to the lower cat. The result of this experiment was that the lower kitten learned to see quite normally, while the upper kitten did not. Most of the upper kittens remained blind or semi-blind. The experiment showed (and Varela's point was) that perception is not passive; it is something you need to enact with your whole body, activating all of your senses.

Today, much of our institutional learning and many of our innovation practices look like the upper cat, which left the legwork to the lower cat. We outsource the legwork to consultants, experts, and trainers. For simple problems that may be fine. But if you are a real innovator, the last thing you want to do is to outsource the legwork of inspiring learning journeys to consultants. You must go there yourself because it is in these connections that the seeds of the future come into the world.

The key is to immerse yourself in the particulars of the field. Studying your customer is not enough. You must **become** your patient, your customer, the marginalized member of your community.

*Company example:* I once facilitated an innovation process for a global automobile manufacturer that focused on improving the self-repair functions of cars. Over a period of two months the team took learning journeys in Europe, Asia, and the United States. When part of the team came to Boston, one of their learning journeys took them to a traditional Chinese medicine (TCM) expert in Cambridge. There they asked how the TCM experts increase the self-healing capacity of the human body. They were told that the body heals differently in different states of awareness: the waking state, the dream state, and the deep-sleep state. Several weeks later, when we met again for the deep-dive retreat, one of the subgroups developed an idea to prototype a dream state for the car. Overnight, the car might run through processes of self-analysis and self-repair, just as the human body does during sleep.

At the conclusion of the workshop, the executive sponsors came in for another day to review the results. They chose this initiative as one of the two most promising and selected it to be prototyped. Today, these self-analysis and self-repair functions are a feature of many cars (including that company's).

*Patient-physician dialogue:* Several years ago in Germany, I worked with a group of students who were investigating the relationships between patients and physicians in their healthcare system. In the reflection period after the students had conducted interviews with 130 patients and their physicians, we were able to identify four levels of relationship between patient and physician (figure 12).

We invited the patients and physicians to a feedback session where we mirrored back to them the different relational qualities they had described. We read them one quote for each level. Then we asked them to discuss in small groups where they saw themselves. Each participant then placed two dots on the drawing of an iceberg that depicted the healthcare system: a black dot to mark their own experience and a white one to mark their desired future.

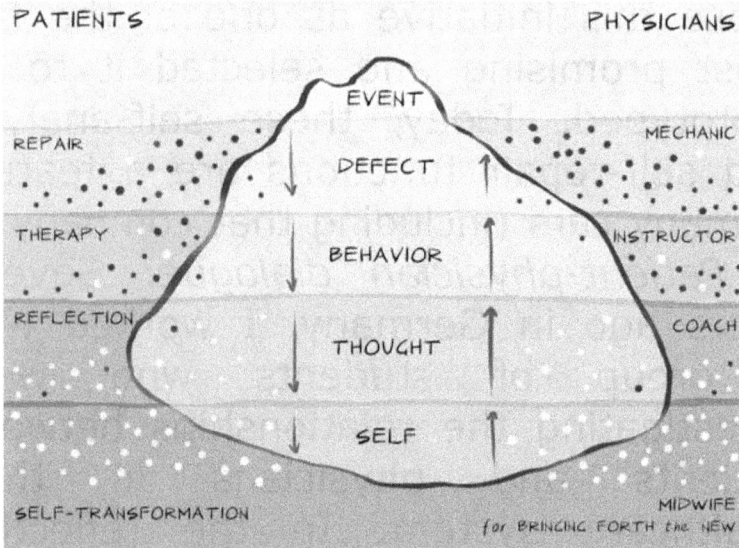

FIGURE 12: Iceberg Model of Patient-Physician Relationships

More than 95 percent of the patients and physicians had placed their black dots on level 1 or 2 and their white dots on level 3 and 4. So I asked them what kept them from operating the way they wanted to. I pointed out that, after all, "**you are** the system." The system was not "them" in Berlin. The system was right there in the room, created by the relationships among them.

You could have heard a pin drop. Then, after the silence, a different kind of conversation emerged. People were more reflective and began asking thoughtful questions. "Why," one of the participants asked, "do we collectively produce results that nobody wants?"

After the physicians openly talked about the pressures and frustrations they experienced, one man stood and introduced himself as the mayor of the town. "What we see in our healthcare system is the same as in politics and government. We always operate on levels 1 and 2. All we do is react to issues and crises, just as we've always done it in the past. But if we operated from those deeper two levels, maybe we could make something different happen." A brief silence followed after the mayor sat down.

Then a woman at the other end of the room stood up and said, "I am a teacher, and I teach in a school nearby, and you know what?" She paused and looked at the mayor and the whole group. "We are facing exactly the same problem. All we do in our schools is to operate on these first two levels." She pointed to the wall with the white and black dots and continued, "We organize our school around mechanical methods of learning. We focus on memorizing the past, on testing old bodies of knowledge, instead of teaching kids how to access their intellectual curiosity and their capabilities for creativity and imagination. We are reacting to crises all the time. And we never succeed in moving our learning environments toward there"—she pointed to levels 3 and 4 on the iceberg chart—"where our kids could learn how to shape their future."

Then the man next to me stood up and said, "I am a farmer, and we are wrestling with exactly the same issue. All we do in conventional agriculture today is tinker with the mechanical issues on levels 1 and 2. We use chemical fertilizers, pesticides, and all kinds of stuff that we drum into the earth, just as you drum a dead body of knowledge into the heads of your students. The whole industrial way of doing agriculture is focused on fighting symptoms and issues with the mechanical solutions of the past. We fail to conceive of our farms and our whole earth as a living organism—as our collective and communal holding space."

Everyone who participated in the conversation that morning felt the presence of a deeper connection. People were not just talking together—they were thinking and feeling together. People talked more slowly, their words punctuated by silence. Something had moved them beyond the usual state where people argue as separate individuals, as captives inside their own brains.

# Outcomes of Co-sensing

Whatever you do in the co-sensing phase, make sure that you generate the following:

1. A revised set of driving forces that reshape the system at issue
2. A revised set of core questions
3. A set of insights into opportunities related to each of them
4. A set of personal connections to these opportunities
5. A core team that is "switched on" to sensing profound opportunities

6. A mapping of the systemic barriers that keep the system on its current track

7. An improved capacity for building generative stakeholder relationships

## *Principles*

### 6. Build a Highly Committed Core Team

It is important for the core team to reflect the diversity of the key stakeholder groups, to bring the talents and competencies needed, and to make the project their number-one priority over the duration of the journey (e.g., four, six, or nine months).

Here is a checklist for a kickoff event that brings the core team together for the first time. To create focus and commitment, clarify:

- What—what you want to create
- Why—why it matters
- How—the process that will get you there
- Who—the roles and responsibilities of all key players involved
- When and where – the road map forward

Additional elements for the kickoff usually include team building; an inspiring speaker who embodies the future; revised driving forces, core questions, and learning journeys; and "mini-training" in dialogue interviews and sensing practices.

## 7. Take Learning Journeys to the Places of Most Potential

Learning journeys connect people to the contexts and ideas that are relevant to creating the possible future. The deep-dive journey moves one's operating perspective from inside a familiar world—the institutional bubble—to an unfamiliar world outside that is surprising, fresh, disturbing, exciting, and new. A deep-dive journey is not a benchmarking trip. It is designed for participants to access a deeper level of emerging reality by observing hands-on practices through total immersion. It incorporates a combination of shadowing, participation, and dialogue.

## 8. Observe, Observe, Observe: Suspend Your Voice of Judgment and Connect with Your Sense of Wonder

Charles Darwin, the father of modern evolutionary theory, was known to keep a notebook with him to capture observations and data that contradicted his theories and expectations. He was well aware that the human mind tends to quickly forget what does not fit into its familiar frameworks.

When the Berlin Wall collapsed in the fall of 1989, Western governments were quick to claim that this event was unexpected and that no one could have anticipated such a geopolitical shift. Was that really true? Just two weeks earlier, Katrin and I had been with an international student group in East Berlin where we talked to representatives of the official system as well as grassroots activists in civil rights movements. During one conversation with members of the opposition movement, the peace researcher Johan Galtung had offered a public wager that the Berlin Wall would collapse by the end of 1989. No member of the opposition movement agreed. We,

Galtung's students, also did not see the evidence that the Eastern European socialist system was about to collapse. We thought that Galtung's prediction was a little off or far-fetched. Well, it wasn't. Why did Galtung, who was exposed to the same data as the rest of us during the trip, emerge with a clear conclusion while we developed a murky "on the one hand, on the other" view?

The primary difference was not the amount of knowledge he had, but a different way of **seeing.** He had a more disciplined way of paying attention. He was able to suspend his habitual judgment and pay closer attention to the reality in front of him.

Only in the suspension of judgment can we open ourselves up to a sense of wonder. Being amazed is about noticing the world beyond downloading. Amazement and wonder are the seeds from which the U process can grow and move us beyond our prison of mental constructs or experiences of the past.

## 9. Practice Deep Listening and Dialogue: Connect with Your Mind and Heart Wide Open

When connecting to other people and contexts, open up all four "channels" of listening: Listen from what you know, from what surprises you, from the whole, and from what you sense wants to emerge (the emerging whole).

I once asked UC Berkeley's Eleanor Rosch, "How can I connect with the whole?" She said, **"Through the heart."** The heart, she explained, "in any contemplative tradition is not an emotionality but a deep yogic centerpoint." The point of deep listening is to use your heart and feelings as organs of perception. It is then, as Rosch puts it, "that the perception begins to happen *from the whole.*"

## 10. Collective Sense Making: Use Social Presencing Theater and Embodied Knowing

Collective sense making of the learning journeys happens in two stages. Stage one is an extended period of disciplined attention to all the experiences and voices of the field. For example, in the debriefing of learning journeys, we often start by asking participants to submit key quotes from their conversations with their stakeholders, which we then hang on the wall, like artwork in a gallery. After a silent walk through the "gallery," the team reflects together and tries to link the themes with their other observations.

Another practice is called Voices from the Field. We sit or stand in a circle and speak from the au then tic voice of the people that we have met. Someone might say, "I am a social entrepreneur, and I have a very clear vision but cannot communicate it well." We do this one by one. Then, when all voices have been heard, the individual participants make entries in their journals about what they have observed and heard, and then take a thirty-minute dialogue walk with a partner, share their observations and reflections with each other, and return to discuss the emerging themes.

Or we sit in a circle and map the entire stakeholder system inside that circle. Then people spontaneously stand up and speak as if they are the stakeholder whose au then tic voice they want to bring into the room. We call this process a "current-reality movie." The only rules are that you cannot step into your own role and that whatever you enact has to reflect your actual experience. With this process you learn how your own role is seen and experienced through the eyes of others.

Whatever process you use to make sense of the learning journey, what matters most is that you pay disciplined attention to all the voices and manifestations of the field, one after another. Paying disciplined attention means that you are intentionally holding back all inclinations to mix in your own interpretations or solutions. You suspend all of that because you want the data of the "field" to speak to you. But the data of the field cannot speak to you if your mind is too busy expressing opinions and proposing solutions.

If stage one of collective sense making is about attending to all the different manifestations of the field, then stage two is where the shift happens.

Stage two is about letting that field, or the mind of the collective, speak to you.

During the second stage we may use various methods and tools, including scenario thinking, systems thinking, and world café. But the most important by far is Social Presencing Theater (SPT). Co-created with and led by my colleague Arawana Hayashi, SPT is a method that blends mindfulness, social science theater, and constellation work. The word "theater" comes from the word root Greek *theatron,* literally "place for viewing" or "to behold." The focus of SPT is on making visible the deep structures of the social field—and how they can evolve.

Two practices are exceptionally helpful during this second stage of the co-sensing movement: 3D mapping (using objects) and 4D mapping (using SPT). These practices are described next and can be found with introductory videos in the free online u.lab course on edx.org and on the Presencing Institute's website. Find direct links to both places at www.presencing.org.

# *Practices*

In our institutions and societies today we have lots of collective downloading mechanisms. But unlike downloading mechanisms, co-sensing mechanisms use the power of shared seeing and dialogue to tap unused resources of collective creativity. In the movement of co-sensing, you do this by engaging in a series of practices described below.

## Practice 1

At the end of each day, spend four minutes in the evening reviewing how you engaged in empathic listening (open mind and heart) and generative listening (open mind, heart, and will). If you cannot identify a single instance of deep listening, take note of that, too. If you do this exercise for a month, your effectiveness as a listener will rise dramatically. All it takes is the discipline to conduct that four-minute review process every day. And if possible, try to find two or three colleagues who will do the same thing and share your experiences with each other. If you cannot find them in your local context, go to www.presencing.org and link up to the u.lab community. U.lab is a free online course that connects people who want to engage with these kinds of practices.

Here is how you differentiate the four levels of listening:

**Listening 1—Habitual:** Your listening happens from what you know, from your inner commentator, not from the person in front of you. Your focus is on reconfirming what you already know.

**Listening 2—Factual:** Your listening focuses on the actual person in front of you. Your inner commentator is fading. You notice what is different. Your focus is on disconfirming data. You see something new.

**Listening 3—Empathic:** Your listening happens from the other person. You begin to see the situation through her eyes. You use your heart as an organ of perception, for tuning into what another person feels, thinks, and wants to say.

**Listening 4—Generative:** Your listening happens from and holds the space for something essential to become present or to manifest. Time slows down, and the boundary between you and the other begins to collapse.

## Practice 2

Choose key stakeholders and conduct a stakeholder dialogue interview in which you put yourself in their shoes and look at your own job from their points of view. Before each interview, engage in a moment of stillness and intention-setting. Here, for example, are four questions that newly promoted directors of a global company use when they interview their stakeholders: their bosses, their customers, their teams, their network:

1. What is your most important objective, and how can I help you realize it? (What do you need me for?)

2. What criteria will you use to assess whether my contribution to your work has been successful?
3. If I were able to change two things in my area of responsibility within the next six months, what two things would create the most value and benefit for you?
4. What, if any, systemic barriers have made it difficult for people in my role or function to fulfill your requirements and expectations? What is getting in our way?

## Practice 3

Learning journeys take us to places of most potential. Ask yourself this: Given the future that you want to create, which people and places are likely to teach you the most about that future and how to make it happen? Deep-dive journeys are usually best when conducted in small groups of up to five people (so that the team can fit into one car). They include the practices of shadowing, dialogue conversations, and, if possible, ongoing activities. The preparation and debriefing are done in a disciplined, structured, and timely fashion. Each team member on a deep-dive journey keeps a journal and uses online tools for real-time documentation and cross-team sharing. Before each visit:

- Gather relevant information about the site you will be visiting.
- Make it clear that you want to talk to/shadow/work with people.
- Prepare a questionnaire as a team (but feel free to deviate from it).
- Conduct a mini-training session on effective observation and sensing practices.
- Prepare a thank-you gift and assign roles (e.g., speaker, timekeeper).
  After each visit:
- Do not check smartphones until the after-action reflection has been completed.
- Plan a time for immediate reflection as a group.
- During this reflection, focus on what you saw and felt.

Here are a few sample questions that you may want to use:

1. What stood out?
2. What was most surprising?
3. What touched my heart?

4. If the organization we visited were a living being, what would it be feeling?
5. If that being could talk, what would it say (to us) now?
6. Moving into and out of this field, what did I notice about myself?
7. What can this field teach us about our possible future?
8. What other ideas does this experience spark for our initiative?

**Practice 4**

A structured process known as 4D mapping is used to map the current reality of an organization's eco-system by going through a mini-U process within a period of three or four hours. While the detailed stages of this method are explained in the SPT section of www.presencing.org, the gist of the method is to:

- Map the current reality with a body constellation or sculpture ("Sculpture 1").
- Morph that constellation or sculpture into a future possibility ("Sculpture 2").
- Debrief the process.

# SPT: Reintegrating Matter and Mind of the Collective

As Arawana Hayashi likes to say, SPT works with the intertwined presence of three bodies. The first one is the Big body: planet earth. The second one is the Small body: our own physical vehicle. The third body is the Social body that we collectively enact.

In most systems we collectively create results that no one wants. Yet it is very difficult to close the knowing-doing gap because we are missing something. We are missing what Peter Senge called the essence of systems thinking: to realign collective behavior (what we do), awareness (what we see), and intention (what we want to see).

*Company examples:* During a workshop we conducted with one of the world's biggest companies, a Chinese state-owned enterprise, people formed what they considered a very harmonious Sculpture 2, with a circle in which everyone faced inward. Everyone could see everyone else. Later, when they reflected on that sculpture, the leadership team was shocked to realize its own blind spot: Nobody was attending to the outside—that is, to the emerging needs of customers and communities. Then the team worked to create five different prototype initiatives, each of which was intended to transform that blind spot in a different domain.

Recently I have worked with two companies in which "customer focus" was considered a key value. But when these companies mapped their Sculpture 1 situation they were surprised to find that their actual practices paid very little attention to their customers. Acknowledging this gap between knowing and doing gave them the shared energy to transform their organization to better embody the customer focus in everyday practices.

In all these cases the intellectual knowledge is not what makes the difference. If I had gone there and told them, "Here is your Sculpture 1 and this is what you should do to get to Sculpture 2," the impact would have been zero. But that is not how SPT works. I just gave them the method, the tools. Then, within half a day, they did it themselves. They created a collective experience of seeing their reality together that will never go away. The mapping functions like a 360-degree scan of the system-wide transformation journey. It gives people a shared language and helps them learn from mistakes even before they make them.

# Presencing: Connecting to the Highest Future Potential

After deeply immersing yourself in the contexts of most potential, the next movement focuses on connecting to your deeper source of knowing—the sources of creativity and Self. Presencing, the blending of sensing and presence, means to operate from the source of one's highest future possibility in the now.

In many ways, presencing resembles co-sensing. Both involve shifting the inner place of operating from the head to the heart. The key difference is that sensing shifts the place of perception to the **current** whole, while presencing shifts the place of perception to the **emerging** future whole.

Michael Ray developed a well-known course on creativity in business at the Stanford Graduate School of Business. Dubbed the "most creative man in Silicon Valley" by Fast Company, he was repeatedly mentioned by the innovators that Joseph Jaworski and I interviewed in 1999. Later that year he agreed to meet us in his office. When we asked him, "How do you help people access their true creativity?" Ray responded, "In all my programs I basically do the same thing. I create a learning environment that allows my participants to address the two root questions of creativity: **Who is my Self?** and **What is my Work?**"

The two questions resonated deeply. "Know thyself" appears in all great wisdom traditions. I remember seeing it inscribed at the entrance to the ancient Greek temple in Delphi. I remember it from studying the teachings of Gandhi in India. And I remember when Master Nan told me in 1999 that in Chinese philosophy, "If you want to be a leader, you have to be a real human being." He also shared his interpretation of Confucius's essay "The Great Learning," which says that **to become a great leader, "you have to cultivate your own opening process."** The full transcript of the interview with Master Nan, "Entering the Seven Meditative Spaces of Leadership," is available at the PI website www.presencing.org.

Presencing uses your higher Self as a vehicle for embodying the future that wants to emerge. The root of the word "presencing," *es,* means "to be." The words *essence, presence,* and *present (gift)* all share this same Indo-European word root. An Old Indian derivative of this same root is *sat,* which means "truth" and "goodness." This term became a major force in the twentieth century when Mahatma Gandhi used it to convey his notion of *satyagraha* (a strategy for finding truth via nonviolent means). An Old German derivative from the same root, *sun,* means "those who are surrounding us" or "the beings who surround us." Presencing connects us to those who surround us.

# *The Presencing Retreat*

The presencing retreat creates a special holding space at the bottom of the U that allows the whole group to connect to their sources of creativity and Self. The retreat takes four or five days and is usually structured as follows: The first stage focuses on sharing and synthesizing the team's findings and identifying themes from their sensing activities. The second stage focuses on a solo experience in nature followed by a debriefing in a sacred circle of sharing. The third stage focuses on crystallizing emerging insights and developing prototyping initiatives.

Over the years, we have found that presencing practices produce a reliable and consistent pattern of profound personal and relational shift. At MIT, I have seen this shift in hundreds of students; and in the projects and programs that I have led around the world, I have seen it in thousands of participants. Everywhere, the personal impact is subtle but profound. But real institutional impact usually requires an intentional and sustained intervention and does not result from merely sending individuals on a retreat.

The prototyping initiatives take time to come to fruition, but when they do, they tend to have profound and lasting impact. It is almost as if the journey to the bottom of the U "switches on" or activates a co-creative social field that, once active, continues to inspire conversations, connections, actions, and ways of thinking together.

# Example from a Global Car Manufacturing Company

For the past twelve years I have worked with one global car manufacturing company, leading a five-day program that helps newly promoted directors deal with their leadership challenges in a context of disruption. The new directors have just moved from leading a single team to leading multiple teams of sometimes thousands or tens of thousands of individuals in complex multi-stakeholder settings across continents, cultures, and reporting lines. In an industry that is going through a much-needed clean energy and transportation disruption, how can I help?

I started designing this program by observing. An organizational development colleague from within the company and I spent four or five days shadowing the new directors. This exercise put us in their shoes and gave us a sense of how lonely it can be to start in a new position without a network of peers.

The participant's journey begins with a one-on-one dialogue with the new directors about their own leadership journeys and current challenges (co-initiating). Then each one conducts dialogue interviews with their top five stakeholders before the workshop begins.

The workshop takes place in a quiet setting with access to nature, not too close to company headquarters. Days one and two are about co-sensing. Participants share their personal and professional contexts with each other and spend most of their time in case clinic groups, using a seven-step process that takes them through the U in about seventy minutes. (Detailed instructions for this process are on the PI website, under Resources.)

Then comes the presencing part of the program (1.5 days), which uses four practices that help participants connect to the two root questions of creativity: Who is my Self? What is my Work? It also includes a half-day silence-in-nature practice.

The third part of the program is about prototyping and performing. With the help of our colleagues from Olivier Mythodrama, we use theater practices to help participants communicate their intentions with a more au then tic leadership presence (co-creating).

The last part of the program is about supporting each other in putting their intentions into practice through small-group peer-coaching video calls (co-shaping).

This intervention works because its intent is different from that of many corporate training programs. The intention of all presencing work is the opposite of corporate indoctrination. It is about increasing, not decreasing, the range of possibilities. It is about strengthening the sources of Self in a world that otherwise tends to tear people apart. It is about making people aware of all their choices and pathways—inside and outside the company—and how to pursue them with curiosity, compassion, and courage.

As a consequence, when the directors return to their jobs, they often feel some distance between their former context (which has not changed) and themselves. That distance does not make their lives easier. It can even be a source of pain (because now they notice the patterns of downloading). But it can also be a source of enhanced awareness and innovation.

## Outcomes of Presencing

Whatever form the presencing movement takes, it should result in the following outcomes:
1. A set of prototyping initiatives
2. Core teams for each prototype initiative
3. A 3D map of each prototype initiative: current reality, future state, leverage points

4.  A list of key stakeholders for each prototype
5.  An inspired energy in the team
6.  A place and support infrastructure for the path forward
7.  A list of potential additional team members that need to be recruited (part-time)
8.  Milestones for reviewing the progress and learning for each prototype
9.  An emerging leadership narrative: the story of us, the story of self, and the story of now (I borrow this last framing from Marshall Ganz of the Harvard Kennedy School)

# Principles

## 11. Circles: Charging the Container

Profound change happens in places, and this place needs to be intentionally created. One of the two best facilitators I know is Beth Jandernoa. She excels at standing in front of a group and, while seeming to do nothing, in an instant establishes a heart-to-heart connection with the whole room. When I asked her how she does this, she said, "It's really very simple. Before I go up front, my practice for over thirty years has been to open my heart and consciously send unconditional love to everyone in the room. It creates a field or surround of love." She credits much of her capacity to be present to a circle of women friends called the Circle of Seven.

I asked Beth if I could interview the Circle of Seven, and they agreed. When they first started meeting in 1995, they had intended to develop a program for women who were going through changes in their professional and personal lives. However, no matter how hard they tried to create an event for others, they kept being redirected to their own lives. Later, the Circle of Seven did create programs for emerging leaders, allowing them to benefit from their experience.

I asked them to explain how the circle practice works. "We always rediscover together how to begin," responded Barbara. "For example, look at what we did at the beginning of this interview," Glennifer explained. "We lit a candle, rang a Tibetan bowl, and went into silence together." During the silence, they may be doing different things internally, she explained. Some listen to what is inside; some listen to the silence. "Our practice is meant to drop us more fully into the field together. Then we move into a deep check-in, giving each other all the time we need to fully bring what each of us is working with in our lives. This charges our space more and more."

Listening to these remarks, I realized that what they described as "charging the space" is quite different from how people normally start a meeting. Usually meetings start with the leader making a presentation or by following a set agenda. In contrast, the Circle of Seven started with the "heart" element of shared experience.

## 12. Letting Go: The Presence of the Circle Being

The biggest obstacle to moving through the bottom of the U comes from within: It emerges from our resistance, from holding on to the past. Moving down the U invites you to suspend your Voice of Judgment, Voice of Cynicism, and Voice of Fear. Dealing with these three forms of resistance requires the cultivation of curiosity, compassion, and courage. Francisco Varela, Eleanor Rosch, and Brian Arthur all emphasize this as the core element of this journey. "Everything that isn't essential must go," Brian Arthur told us when he described his experience of crossing this threshold.

Two major elements need to come together to activate the generative field. The first one has to do with **charging the container,** with unconditional love and listening without judgment and cynicism. The second has to do with courage, vulnerability, **letting go,** and surrender.

As my conversation with the Circle of Seven continued, Glennifer said: "This may not be true for others, but for me it's so hard to release my personal boundary and relax into the circle. It takes a huge amount of inner work and letting go for me to do that. Each of us works differently with how we let go into the collective. Each time it requires crossing a threshold."

I asked Glennifer what it was like to cross the threshold. She said, "I feel as though I'm going to die if I let myself go into the circle. So I have to notice and be okay with that feeling. Crossing that boundary is what I imagine it must feel like to die. Who will I be? Because I don't know, I'm not sure how to protect myself." I wanted to know, "So what happens next?" Glennifer said, "Then I usually step over the boundary. If I step all the way, it's such a relief to have taken the step. I feel freer. Somehow I didn't know beforehand that I would feel freer, even though I've done it before.

"When everyone's done that," she continued, "we have this collective presence in a different way. We have a new being—the presence of the Circle Being. My experience is that until I've done that, I don't experience the Circle Being. After that, it's beyond me as an individual. I don't matter so much as an individual anymore. Yet, paradoxically, I'm more of an individual at the same time."

"What I saw happening was that you took a risk," another member of the

Circle of Seven said. "There has to be a risk in order for the collective to show up. The risk can be one person's, two persons', or all of ours, but there has to be some kind of risk or vulnerability associated with crossing the threshold that you're talking about. I felt the whole space shift. Because you took a risk, it shifted the space for all of us." You can find the full transcript of the Circle of Seven interview on the PI website (www.presencing.org).

## 13. Intentional Silence: Pick a Practice That Helps You Connect with Your Source

The currency that counts at the bottom of the U is not ideas, words, or insights. Here you must use a different currency: **practice.** Practice is what we do every day. Thus this principle is about picking a personal practice that will help you connect to your future resonance. There are many practices available (examples given below). You have to find and modify your own.

## 14. Follow Your Journey: Do What You Love, Love What You Do

Michael Ray of Stanford University frames this principle as "Do what you love, love what you do." His motto captures what I have heard many successful creators and innovators say: To access your best creativity, you have to go on a journey—a journey in which you follow your bliss, your feeling, your felt sense of an emerging future. You must trust that sense more than all the good advice you get from other people, which may also be valuable.

For example, even if you do not love your work, make sure that you have at least one or two projects in your portfolio of activities that have that quality of the heart. They will help you to activate the deeper capacities of your creativity which then radiate into the rest of your work and life.

What it all boils down to is this: Whenever you make important decisions, never underestimate the voice of your heart. It is a quality of feeling that you can tune in to and that is evoked by a situation. It tells you a lot about the field. Whenever I have followed it at important crossroads, it has pointed me down the right path.

## 15. Letting Come: Presencing the Future Wanting to Emerge

The essence of the U is that, instead of projecting your small will—"Me First"—you relax, let go, and let come your emerging or "grand will" (Buber), shifting from me to we, from ego to eco.

We have experienced these kinds of shifts time and again in our work with leaders after they engaged with the intelligence of the social field. In the presencing movement we usually use a variety of practices. Just as different people have different learning styles, different practices work for different people. So offering different pathways into the sacred territory is key.

# *Practices*

## Practice 1: Morning Practice

Try to start your day intentionally, by ignoring your smartphone. Many of us keep our phones next to our bed, which makes it likely that we check messages and email right before going to sleep and right after waking up. That is about the worst thing we can do because it disconnects us instantly from the subtle echo and resonance of the night. The goal is to stay with that body of resonance, not to lose it right away, to begin the day by attending to your deeper levels of knowing.

Here is one way to do a morning practice (ten to thirty minutes):

- Rise early (before the others in your house hold), go to a place of silence that works for you (a place in nature is great, but you also may find other places that work for you), and allow your inner knowing to emerge.
- Use a ritual that connects you with your source. It can be meditation, prayer, or simply an intentional silence that you enter into with an open heart and open mind.
- Remember what brought you to the place in life where you are right now. Who is your Self? What is your Work? What are you here for?
- Make a commitment to what you want to be in service of on this day.

- Feel appreciation for the opportunity to live the life that you have right now.
- Ask for help so that you do not lose your way or get sidetracked.

Regardless of our profession, after that first hour of the day, most of us face the same situation: disruption and unexpected challenges. It is a part of living in this century. The question is how to deal with it. Panic? React? Get defensive? Or can you meet these challenges from a different place that is grounded in the future that you want to create?

## Practice 2: Holding Space

"If we have a dominant circle practice," explained Anne, another member of the Circle of Seven, "it has to do with holding." The women described three conditions of listening that enable a collective holding space to emerge.

The first one they call **"unconditional witnessing."** According to Anne, "The quality of witnessing or holding that we're talking about here is identification with the source in the circle. Something like: the eyes through which you see, the heart through which you feel, the ears with which you listen are not personal. So there is very little projection onto the situation. There is little intent other than opening to what life wants to have happen right then. There's sensitivity without manipulation. A spirit of nonjudgment and blessing."

The second one is **"unconditional love."** "The focus of energy drops out of the head and into the heart in the room, because the opening usually happens when somebody's heart really opens, and definitely when the field is identified. The energy field has to drop. There is a blessing that comes with impersonal love," Anne explained.

The third condition is **"seeing the essential self."** Noted Barbara, "I see through that wound to the truth of her. So it's where I place my awareness that does the work. It's a discipline of attention that has to do with how I see the people who are described by others in the circle." Leslie added, "We have an agreement to see the essential self that we call the no-mess-up clause. No matter what one of us does, she can't mess up as far as the others are concerned. So the intention is placed on the essential self. We have a shared belief that one of the greatest forms of service to people is to see their essential selves—that somehow through my seeing that, they experience more of themselves."

"This may be my own attribution," said Glennifer, "but here's how I experience work in the Circle, if I'm the one who's doing the work, being witnessed, or assisted by another person. My experience is that there's a thickness in the atmosphere—an enabling presence—that allows me to go deeper than if, say, Beth and I were working only with one another.... I see more. I see more of myself. I see more of what I'm working with. Now, I don't know whether that's because of the skill levels in the group or whether it's because of the quality of attention or a combination of both. But my experience is that I see more; I experience more of myself.

"I feel like a bigger person. I feel fuller in my own being," Glennifer added. "And I feel empowered or enabled in a particular way. I feel seen. I feel the focus of attention is fine; that it's qualitative, nonjudgmental, and loving. And I feel the presence of the Circle Being, which is different from the sum of the individuals."

# Transforming the Shadows of Berlin

Moments of presencing happen on their own schedule, not necessarily on ours. We learned that during our advanced practitioner program at the Presencing Institute. In the last module of this two-year program, seventy-two participants from nineteen countries met in Berlin. My friend and colleague Dayna Cunningham remembers a profound moment of transformation from the meeting that demonstrates how all the aspects of presencing come together.

"Several of our group, with a Jewish background, had lost family during the Holocaust," remembers Dayna, "while other members of our group came from a German background. Spending a week together in Berlin, and visiting, among other places, the Holocaust Memorial, brought back painful and yet important memories to many.

"The next day, our group of seventy-two change makers experienced a profound shift of the field that allowed Jews, Germans, Americans, Asians, Africans, Latin Americans, and Australians to connect to each other and to themselves on a much deeper, more raw, and more vulnerable and essential level than any of us had experienced in such a group before.

"Otto opened the conversation by bringing us back to the experience of being in Berlin. It was emotional for him, and his willingness to be raw and vulnerable opened a crack. Suddenly many people were sharing their own personal stories. One story shared by Gail Jacob, an American Jewish woman, deeply touched me," Dayna said. "Her mother, a death camp survivor, had faced unspeakable horrors in the camp, but the only memory she had shared with her children was of seeing Germans weeping as they lined the streets outside the camp when it was liberated. For me, it was breathtaking that she chose only to highlight the humanity of a people whose country had committed such atrocities against her.

"As the stories unfolded, the listening in the room dropped deeper and an incredible conversation started to take its course—a shift of the field that allowed each of us to see our life's journey from a different and more collective angle. There was a flow experience of speaking from the core, speaking from what is moving through me and through us. Many of the stories were about intense personal suffering, but in the room, held by the collective listening and light, they were transformed into moments of powerful healing."

One of the Jewish participants, Yishai Yuval from Israel, remembered the situation like this: "[At the being of the conversation] people stood up and talked on suffering, cruelty, and the need to remember. I looked around at my fellow Jews in the room, expecting them to join the conversation. At the beginning none did. It hit me that this type of discussion can't go on while the victims' voice is missing. So, contrary to my habit, I raised my hand to ask for the microphone. The ten steps from the corner where I was sitting into the group's circle were a very long journey....

"What happened was a personal defining moment," Yishai said. "Everything slowed down around me. There was no need to struggle with words and sentences. They just came one by one in the right order. I felt the faces around me listening, radiating profound empathy, deep understanding, and love. It became easy to share with the group the notion that, prior to being exterminated, Holocaust victims struggled day after day to maintain their dignity as human beings in the midst of the surrounding horrors.

"Many of them realized that humanity and love didn't save them, concluding that anger, aggressiveness, even hatred, might do better in that daily struggle for survival. As an Israeli, this is the heritage I was born into. One can count only on oneself to be strong and suspicious. I was proud as a soldier, trained to kill if necessary, blessed for protecting my own family and people; blessed for not being helpless; blessed for not being in the mercy of brutal killers like my mother's parents and sister. But time moved on and suddenly we, Israelis, have the power over other people [and are] forced to face annoying questions: Are we strong enough not to exercise power and still remain safe? Had the time arrived to put aside suspicions and hatred, open our hearts, and offer real peace with our enemy?"

Yishai went on: "As I talked, looking around the circle I felt I belonged and was connected to the whole. The deep listening and empathy radiated around me well after I stepped out of the circle. A little while later a young Jewish American woman stood up at the opposite corner of the big hall, asking just to sing a piece written by a young, brave Jewish woman who left Palestine in 1944, parachuted into Hungary on a rescue mission, but was caught by the Nazis, tortured, and killed.

"Hearing her gentle voice singing so emotionally, I couldn't resist standing up, at the other side of the hall, and joining her. Since then, whenever I hear that song I tremble inside. It touches me in unknown land, in a way unrecognized to me before. I'll never forget that precious moment of connection with that wonderful young woman as well as with the whole group."

Shortly after that, Tho Ha Vinh of Vietnam and Bhutan stood up and shared a poem by Thich Nhat Hanh. The name of the poem is "Call Me by My True Names," said Tho, as he reached into his pocket to pull out a small journal that helped him to keep this poem close to his heart. Tho started reading:

> *Do not say that I'll depart*
> *tomorrow because even today I*
> *still*
> *arrive.*
>
> *...*
>
> *I am the frog swimming happily in*
> *the clear pond,*
> *and I am also the grass-snake*
> *who, approaching in silence,*
> *feeds itself on the frog.*
>
> *I am the child in Uganda, all skin*
> *and bones,*

*my legs as thin as bamboo sticks,*
*and I am the arms merchant,*
*selling deadly*
*weapons to Uganda.*

*I am the twelve-year-old girl,*
*refugee on a*
*small boat,*
*who throws herself into the ocean*
*after being*
*raped by a sea pirate,*
*and I am the pirate, my heart not*
*yet capable*
*of seeing and loving.*
*...*

*Please call me by my true names,*
*so*
*I can wake up,*
*and so the door of my heart can*
*be*
*left open,*
*the door of compassion.*

Total stillness. Tho sat down. We all felt the walls between us melting away. Time slowed down and our own experience of that moment was elevated. We started experiencing the situation from multiple angles. I am the girl. The pirate. I am in you. You are in me. I am in We. We is in me.

"What struck me most deeply," remembers Dayna, "was the level of connection and compassion people expressed toward others who had been life-and-death adversaries or who had done violence to them: the soldiers, survivors of assault and neglect, the Jewish descendants of Holocaust survivors and the young Germans." Gail, another Jewish American member of our group, adds: "I am sixty-three years old. I've spent my whole life as a Jew thinking I was alone in this world, thinking that if anything happened to me or my people, no one would help. Now in this room in Berlin, I understand that I am not alone."

Never before had I experienced such a profound transformation on the level of the collective. It felt as if many of the long, dark shadows of the collective past finally rose to the surface, in order to be released and transubstantiated into energy and light. The group functioned as the holding space.

So what enabled this shift to happen? Here are the two conditions that we discussed in the context of the Circle of Seven.

The first condition is **the quality of the container and holding space.** The holding space that was created in Berlin had started to form six months earlier in a small coaching-circle gathering. Each participant in the advanced program had met monthly in a small "group of seven" for two years. Gail remembered: "When we met in our coaching group six months earlier, I shared my trepidation about going [to Berlin] and using that as an opportunity to visit where I was born—the displaced persons' camp near Dachau, from which both my parents were liberated.

"Before I knew what I was going to say, I was talking about going to Berlin and taking my family to where I was born for the first time. I started crying and then the group wept together for a long time and there was this amazing knowing in the group about healing—not only me, but knowing also how the world needs to heal from our collective trauma of war and genocide.

"There I was sitting next to Otto, a German, and two Buddhists—Tho, a Vietnamese; Julia, of Korean descent—also Yishai, an Orthodox Israeli Jew; Jim, a former military person from the U.S.; and Antoinette, the next generation.... They were able to be my holding space.... I felt the earth shift. I've carried the wounds of the Holocaust in my DNA and in my being every day of my life. Somehow for the first time I began to see the possibility of transforming that energy into something else.

"The field shifted during that morning with the class," remembers Gail, referring to the quality of the holding space. "We were open to each other and we were one. It was as though **collectively we needed to embrace the shadow** in order to glimpse what is needed to heal the world. And for me, the fear was gone."

The second condition of possibility was people's **willingness to go to the edge of the abyss, to let go of fear**—and take the leap into the unknown.

When Yishai, against his nature, took the microphone, he took that leap. So did Gail and many others. The same applied to me, when I started opening the space. When I sensed that something wanted to happen, which started days before and intensified as we came closer, it first felt as if I was going to die. But then, the presence of our coaching circle, the directly felt connection to Gail, Yishai, Tho, and the others, allowed me to let go of the fear and make a move toward what wanted to happen, just as Yishai and Gail described. The collective space that opened up was so much higher and deeper than I was able to grasp.

# Co-creating: Crystallizing and Prototyping the New

The aim of co-creating is to build landing strips for the future through prototypes that allow us to explore the future by doing. The prototypes evolve based on the feedback they generate. The "observe, observe, observe" of the co-sensing phase becomes "iterate, iterate, iterate." This movement is inspired by design thinking and blended with presencing principles to make it relevant to profound shifts in social fields.

# Examples from Namibia and Brazil

*Namibia:* With our partners at Synergos and with the help of McKinsey and Company, we co-facilitated a public sector healthcare lab in Namibia. We took a small cross-sector group of leaders, including nurses, doctors, and the regional director, on all of the different sensing journeys. The goal was to improve maternal health. During the prototyping stage they focused on four separate initiatives. The feedback they received eventually produced a fifth prototype that became the most successful of all. It resulted in the idea of Regional Delivery Units (RDUs) that would allow them to accelerate innovation and learning among stakeholders that previously operated in institutional silos, disconnected from each other.

The weekly cross-organizational RDU meeting began with a review of the week's data and events, during which professionals of different ranks questioned each other and exchanged views in a supportive and nonjudgmental environment. At one RDU team meeting I attended, they discussed a situation of concern to the nurses. A junior female nurse turned to the most senior (male) leader at the table (the regional director), who had not participated in the discussion up to that point. She said: "I gather from your body language that you do not agree with what is being said here." And then it was the director's turn to explain his reading of the situation. When I heard that junior nurse draw out the most senior person in the group (across status, profession, and gender), I knew that something was working—they had established a constructive communication and learning culture.

*Brazil:* In developing the Food and Nutrition Lab in Brazil, Denise Chaer started with forty organizations and people from all sectors of the food delivery system—grassroots organizers, representatives of city and national governments, academics, and multinational food companies. Their task was to co-create prototype initiatives to address their complex systemic challenges. The group scaled down to thirty participants to begin the prototyping work. Participants developed their ideas across sectoral and organizational boundaries. After two months of working in the self-organized prototyping groups, the facilitation team invited all the teams back to a reflection workshop, in which five prototypes emerged as the most promising.

One team formed a coalition among Coca-Cola, Ambev, and Pepsi that resulted in the official announcement in 2015 that they would stop selling sugary drinks in school canteens to children under age twelve starting that same year. In addition, the companies agreed to stop all advertising targeted at children throughout Brazil. Another initiative created "Fonte da Juventude," a documentary series on national TV that helps children understand the need for fruits and vegetables in their diet. Since then, the participants have also created an organic farming lab and a leadership lab.

A critical juncture in the prototyping process always is the first feedback session. This session happens about six weeks after the presencing retreat. Each team presents what they have learned from their sensing activities and their stakeholders and their ideas for going forward. Then they get more rounds of feedback and iterate their ideas accordingly.

# Outcomes of Co-creating

1. A set of refined prototypes—living microcosms of the future—that have generated meaningful feedback regarding the guiding questions and objectives of the lab
2. A set of connections with stakeholders and partners that are relevant for taking the prototype to pilot and scale
3. Enhanced leadership and innovation capacities for dealing with disruptive innovation

4.  A team spirit that could help change the leadership culture in the company
5.  Creative confidence among the team members to take on big and complex projects

## Principles

### 16. The Power of Intention: Crystallize Your Vision and Intent

Nick Hanauer founded half a dozen highly successful companies and was a board member of Amazon for many years. When Joseph Jaworski and I interviewed him, he was working with a small group of people to "reinvent" the educational system in the state of Washington. When we asked about the role of intention in his entrepreneurial experience, Hanauer replied, "One of my favorite sayings, attributed to Margaret Mead, has always been 'Never doubt that a small group of thoughtful, committed citizens can change the world. Indeed, it's the only thing that ever has.' I totally believe it. **You could do almost anything with just five people.** With only one person, it's hard—but when you put that one person with four or five more, you have a force to contend with. I think that's what entrepreneurship is all about—creating that compelling vision and force."

## 17. Form Core Groups: Five People Can Change the World

Nick Hanauer's view may seem a bit too American, male, and "tech entrepreneur" – centric. Yet, I believe he is right. Whenever I have seen or participated in a profound episode of change, it always boils down to the same core phenomenon: a small group of people who are deeply committed to a shared purpose and intent. It might take a few more than five people to change the world. But that core group radiates an intention to the world that has the power to attract people, opportunities, and resources that make things happen. Then momentum builds. The core group functions as a vehicle for the whole to manifest.

## 18. Create a Platform or Place

Innovation happens in places. In nature, before the caterpillar transforms into a butterfly, it needs the shelter of the cocoon. Cocooning is a key activity of the creative process; the cocoon is the holding space that is needed for profound innovation. Also incorporate a "milestone structure" that forces the team to produce prototypes early on and generates fast-cycle feedback from stakeholders. Build in access to help from peers and experts that enables the team to go through the rapid-learning U cycle almost every day.

## 19. Build a 0.8 Prototype

A prototype is a microcosm of the future that you want to create. Prototyping means to present your idea (or work in progress) before it is fully developed. The purpose of prototyping is to generate feedback from all stakeholders about how it looks, how it feels, how it matches (or does not match) people's needs and aspirations, and then to refine the assumptions about the guiding project. The focus is on exploring the future by doing rather than by analyzing. As the folks at IDEO have put it, the rationale for prototyping is "to fail often to succeed sooner" or to **"fail early to learn quickly."**

A prototype is not a plan. It is something you do that generates feedback. But a prototype is also not a pilot. A pilot has to be a success; by contrast, a prototype may fail, but it focuses on maximizing learning.

At Cisco Systems, a world leader in networking equipment, the prototyping imperative begins with what that company calls principle 0.8: Regardless of how long term the project, engineers are expected to come up with a first prototype within three or four months—otherwise the project is dead. The first prototype is not expected to work like a 1.0 prototype—it is a quick-and-dirty iteration that generates feedback from all key stakeholders.

## 20. Iterate, Iterate, Iterate: Always Be in Dialogue with the Universe

Do not get stuck on the initial form of your idea. Always learn from the feedback of the universe. Hone and iterate your idea using each interaction.

This principle has been effectively described and framed by Alan Webber, the co-founder of Fast Company. As he notes, "The universe actually is a helpful place. If you're open in relation to your idea, **the universe will help you.** It wants to suggest ways for you to improve your idea. Now, that said, the universe sometimes offers suggestions that suck. Part of the adventure is listening to those ideas and suggestions and trying to make your own calculations about which ones are helpful and which ones are harmful."

## 21. Seek It with Your Hands: Integrate Head, Heart, and Hand

As the master coach puts it in the novel and 2000 movie *Bagger Vance* when helping a golfer who has lost his swing: "Seek it with your hands—don't think about it, feel it. The wisdom in your hands is greater than the wisdom of your head will ever be."

This is of course what artists have always known. Erik Lemcke, a sculptor and management consultant from Denmark, once shared with me his experience:

> After having worked with a particular sculpture for some time, there comes a certain moment when things are changing. When

this moment of change comes, it is no longer me, alone, who is creating. I feel connected to something far deeper, and my hands are co-creating with this power. At the same time, I feel that I am being filled with love and care as my perception is widening. I sense things in another way. It is a love for the world and for what is coming. I then intuitively know what I must do. **My hands know** if I must add or remove something. My hands know how the form should manifest. In one way, it is easy to create with this guidance. In those moments I have a strong feeling of gratitude and humility.

My hands know. That is the key to operating on the right-hand side of the U. Moving down the left-hand side of the U is about opening up and dealing with the resistance of thought, emotion, and will. Moving up the right-hand side is about intentionally reintegrating the intelligences of the head, the heart, and the hand in the context of practical applications.

Just as the inner enemies on the way down the U deal with the Voice of Judgment, the Voice of Cynicism, and the Voice of Fear, the barriers on the way up the U are the three disconnected ways of operating:

- **Mindless action:** executing without learning
- **Action-less mind:** analysis paralysis
- **Blah-blah-blah:** oversharing, talking without embodied change

The three barriers share the same structural feature: Instead of balancing the intelligence of the head, heart, and hand, one dominates (the *head* in analysis paralysis; the *will* in mindless action; and the *heart* in oversharing).

The prototyping pentagon in figure 13 summarizes the six principles of co-creating. When moving into the stage of prototyping, pay attention to them.

# Practices

## Practice 1: Listen to the Voice of the Future

Physicist and educator Arthur Zajonc developed this practice, which he describes as follows. "I'll be in a board meeting where the energy is tough and maybe I'm up against some hot issue. I don't know how to deal with it. I find myself in those times letting go. It's a practice of saying, 'Okay, we've had full, bloody attention on this thing. We've really turned over a lot of stuff.' Then I kind of sit back and expand in nonfocal awareness. Empty out. Sometimes I even pretend there's an invisible person next to me.

"When I was chairing the board of a new school, sometimes I would imagine invisible children at the table. I was actually working for these children who were not yet born or were not yet there. They were my reason for being there. I try to listen into the space. The future is also at the table. There is a wonderful creative moment when everyone present recognizes a special moment. I encourage them to hold on to it, to play it out. Those moments give a lot of positive energy to a group," Zajonc says. "There's a feeling of originality, can-do, and collaboration. Nobody takes owner ship because the idea could have come from somebody else across the table."

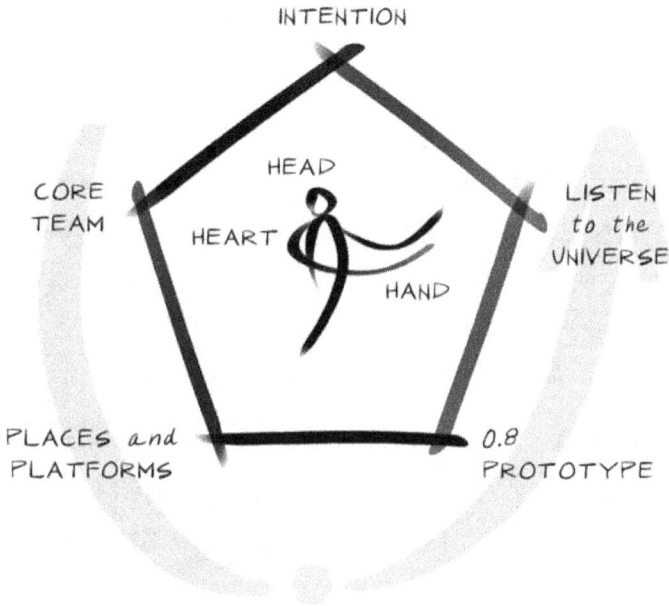

FIGURE 13: The Pentagon of Prototyping

## Practice 2: Listen to the Universe

Step 1: Take three minutes at the end of each day to write down the suggestions the world has made to you that day, without judging them as good or bad.

Step 2: Write down one or two questions that follow from those suggestions that relate to current challenges in your work.

Step 3: The next morning, take five or ten minutes to write down the answers to the questions you put on paper the night before. If a stream of ideas comes through, go with the flow.

Step 4: Complete the "journaling" by exploring the possible next steps: What would it take to further investigate, test, or prototype your ideas?

This practice offers a safe place in which to explore new or challenging ideas and will significantly increase your capacity to read weak signals and develop your thinking.

## Practice 3: Select Ideas for Prototyping

Ask these seven "R" questions as you select and evolve an idea for prototyping:

1. **Is it *relevant?*** Does it matter to the stakeholders involved? Is it truly relevant individually (for the persons involved), institutionally (for the organizations involved), and socially (for the communities involved)?

2. **Is it *revolutionary?*** Is it new? Is it transformative to the system?

3. **Is it *rapid?*** Can you do it quickly? Can you develop

experiments right away with enough time to get feedback and adapt (and thus avoid analysis paralysis)?

4. **Is it *rough?*** Can you do it on a small scale? Can you do it at the lowest possible resolution that allows for meaningful experimentation? Can you do it locally, to let the local context teach you how to get it right?

5. **Is it *right?*** Can you see the whole in the microcosm that you are focused on? Does this idea allow you to put the spotlight on the most critical variables? You have to choose your focus so that you can see the core issue of the system. You cannot, for example, ignore the patients in a health study, the consumers in a sustainable food project, or the students in a school project.

6. **Is it *relationally effective?*** Does it leverage the strengths, competencies, and resources of the existing networks and communities?

7. **Is it *replicable?*** Can you scale it? Any innovation in business or society hinges on its replicability

and whether it can grow to scale. In the context of prototyping, these criteria favor approaches that activate local participation and owner ship and exclude those that depend on massive infusions of external knowledge, capital, and owner ship.

# Co-shaping: Grow Innovation Eco-systems

The movement of co-shaping focuses on scaling the new while growing and evolving innovation eco-systems for collective impact.

The problem with today's societal eco-systems is the broken feedback loop between the parts and the whole. The essence of consciousness-based systems thinking, aka Theory U, is to relink the parts and the whole by making the system sense and see itself—by **closing the feedback loop between collective impact and shared awareness.** At the end of the day, all of the application stories in this book rely on this one methodological backbone.

It is why the innovation labs are working; it is why their initiatives have been able to succeed. But what about the larger eco-systems in which they—and all of us—operate?

That is where these new innovation infrastructures for making the system sense and see itself are largely missing. The lack of these infrastructures is one of the biggest barriers to societal innovation today.

The reason this matters is that we are in the midst of seeing the birth of a fourth coordination mechanism. We are all familiar with the three traditional mechanisms that coordinate our social and economic systems: hierarchies, markets, and negotiations among organized interest groups (chapter 3).

But we know that these three means on their own will not be able to provide the upgrade of our governance mechanisms that is called for today. Therefore the emerging fourth coordination mechanism is critical: **acting from shared awareness**—acting from seeing the whole. The development of that collective capacity requires cultivation, practice, and enabling infrastructures. And that is what this fifth movement of the U, co-shaping, is about.

Let us begin by talking about the prototypes. Each prototype goes through many iterations. As it evolves, it retains the best features of its earlier forms but changes in other ways in order to improve. The next question is: How can we use what we learn in these small-scale experiments and apply it to the evolution of the whole?

If you have ever been in a live theater production, you know that the actors get input from one another as well as guidance from the director, and the performance benefits from that refining process. Things are added; things are removed. Theater is a living structure—contained, honed, and refined. Only after many rehearsals is the curtain ready to go up. And still it evolves, but now with the added component of the audience's energy and presence.

# Examples from Namibia and the MITx u.lab

*Namibia:* The RDU prototype team processes were rolled out throughout Namibia's thirteen regions. The purpose was not to implement the specific healthcare outcomes of the prototype, but to implement the process and structure. Each region could then modify the approach to fit its specific regional health context. The work is now owned by and performed for Namibians, without any international partners. The RDU process makes the leaders accountable for improving outcomes. The teams drive policy implementation, coordinate service delivery, manage progress on goals, and solve problems to ensure the effectiveness of health interventions. According to our partners at Synergos (www.synergos.org), who co-facilitated the healthcare lab in Namibia, the new system has contributed to lowering infant and maternal mortality by about 14 percent between 2006 and 2013.

The success of the RDU prototype depended on three enabling conditions:

1. The creation of an institutional infrastructure to produce usable data
2. The establishment of a cross-organizational structure that regularly convenes key players from across institutional silos to analyze the data
3. The development of a learning culture that allows people to innovate instead of blaming each other

These three conditions also proved to be important in the coshaping or scaling phase. Their application in each specific context gave rise to a whole eco-system of RDUs with different yet similar ways of operating.

*MITx u.lab:* My view of how innovations can be brought to scale has shifted profoundly. Until 2015, my colleagues and I at the Presencing Institute were busy running projects and programs in various parts of the world—on sustainable business, food and farming, health and well-being, finance, learning and leadership, and government and governance. Each one operated in a different sociopolitical and geographic context.

How did all of this hang together? It did not. Until 2015. Then something happened that turned this set of isolated projects and programs into a vibrant field of global connection. "It is as if something got inverted," said Katie Stubley, our PI colleague from Western Australia. "Suddenly everyone could feel the living field of global connection that we all are part of."

The turning point was the launch of our u.lab MOOC. Massive open online courses have disrupted the traditional way of delivering education and democratized access to knowledge and learning. However, MOOCs have also been criticized for having low completion rates and for a low-quality learning environment (sitting in front of a computer screen).

The purpose of the u.lab experiment was to answer this question: Can an online-to-offline learning environment blend the **democratization of knowledge** with **activating the deep learning cycle** (head, heart, hand)?

We learned that, yes, it is possible, but it takes a complex holding space and structure to make it work, including case clinic circles, local hubs, and live sessions that bring together the global community and make it possible for them to sense and see themselves. We were able to scale up quickly because we had already prototyped all of these elements individually. But we had never put them together. And that is very much a core theme in co-shaping: letting your ecosystem evolve by better blending and linking the elements and the whole.

## Outcomes of Co-shaping

1. Reviewing prototype initiatives
2. Sharing key learnings
3. Deciding which prototypes/ideas to advance to the pilot phase
4. Widening the focus from prototype to evolving the ecosystem as whole
5. Infrastructures that allow the eco-system to see itself
6. A set of bottlenecks that, if removed, allowed the new to go to scale

7. Newly formed generative partnerships and alliances for scaling the new
8. A new narrative that links the work with societal or civilizational renewal

## *Principles*

### 22. Create Enabling Infrastructures That Allow the System to Sense and See Itself

Here are two examples. The first example is from the world of finance. RSF Social Finance, a social impact investing organization based in San Francisco, regularly convenes its investors and borrowers to learn about each other's contexts and then jointly determine the interest rate that borrowers will pay investors over the next period. Don Shaeffer, CEO of RSF Social Finance, says "These conversations have their own magic. What happens is not what you think would happen. You would think that investors would argue for higher and borrowers argue for lower rates. But that's not what happens. It is often the exact opposite.

"It's an interesting process, and we are still learning how to best hold the space for that."

The second example is from the world of health. One widely used method of reducing mistakes in hospitals has been the introduction of checklists. Research shows that the introduction of checklists in hospitals at first lowers the risk of mistakes, but gradually the error rate returns to near its former level. Noticing that pattern, Dr. Marc Parnes, an OB/GYN surgeon in Ohio, devised a different practice. Instead of using a checklist, he converses directly with patients as they are rolled into the procedure room. They have a quick personal "check-in conversation" that includes the patient and the entire operating team. Surprisingly, this check-in practice reduces the rate of errors in a more sustainable way than the simple checklist practice without a face-to-face conversation.

These two examples demonstrate how "making the system sense and see itself" can change the coordination dynamics among the players in a field, moving them toward eco-system awareness. But what about larger systems? How can similar practices be applied on a regional, national, or even global level?

## 23. Create Massive Capacity-Building Mechanisms

Two things that are missing in society today are (1) infrastructures for seeing from the whole and (2) massive capacity-building mechanisms for co-sensing and co-creating future possibilities.

Practice fields are the key to building that capacity. No symphony orchestra or professional soccer or basketball team can achieve world-class excellence without practicing. Likewise, leaders and change makers need tools and practice fields in which to learn to use their tools effectively. Once we conducted a project with FedEx, the international courier service. Every night hundreds of airplanes and millions of parcels fly in and out of their hubs, where each package is sorted according to its destination within approximately two hours. To manage this logistical miracle the company runs four after-action reviews every day. Four times a day they focus on what they are learning and what can be improved. If you do that for a decade or two, you become a world-class logistics company. On a society level, these types of infrastructures are largely missing.

## 24. Labs and Platforms for Cultivating the Social Soil

While meeting with a leading venture philanthropist in Silicon Valley, I shared with her my vision for a u.school—how the u.lab could evolve into a global action research university that cultivates the social soil in a variety of ways. When I was finished, she responded: "You know, it's not easy to fundraise for this. Most high-net-worth people around here do not like to give away their money. So they don't. And if they do it," she said, "they only do it under three conditions: one, technology is the solution; two, the problem can be measured and solved within ten years; and three, the donor can call the shots."

Those three points beautifully sum up everything that is wrong with philanthropy and impact investing today. The first condition excludes the entire universe of systemic challenges that need more than a technology fix. The second condition excludes all issues that can only be shifted over the long term—which is just about anything of real importance. And the third condition reveals a lack of understanding of generative capital.

In my experience, platforms that cultivate the social field need (a) an initial endowment that sets the tone, such as shared intellectual capital but also other forms of capital, and (b) the establishment of a community that keeps generating the field of co-creativity.

In the first part of the book I identified the intertwined dynamics of two social fields—presencing and absencing—as a key characteristic of our time. All of us know examples of both in our direct environment. But when it comes to macro and mundo structures, we see massive amplification mechanisms for absencing (in the form of media and social media), but almost no amplification of presencing.

This brings us to cultivating the social soil on a large scale. To explore how this can be done, in early 2018 the Presencing Institute and HuffPost will launch a joint initiative: an interactive multimedia hub, designed as a hybrid between media and movement building. It will combine quality journalism focused on the new economic narrative—examples that embody principles and practices for transforming capitalism—with a new "u.lab-type" learning platform that blends methods, tools, live-sessions, global mindfulness moments, and deeply personal small group dialogues. Users will be offered various pathways of engagement, ranging from conversations with peers to self-organized sensing journeys to discover the seeds of the new economy locally, and change makers will find tools that help to move their initiative from idea to action. The objective is to create a platform that helps this emerging global movement become aware of itself. (You can find this platform at www.presencing.org.)

# PART III

# A Narrative of Evolutionary Societal Change

Theory U is three things (1) a framework, (2) a method, and (3) a movement. What I mean by movement is a new narrative of social, economic, and cultural evolution that applies to all sectors and systems, and that aims at bridging the ecological, social, and spiritual divides. This final part briefly outlines such an evolutionary view (which, if fully spelled out, would be a whole other book). It applies the Theory U lens to the evolution of societal systems.

With these two closing chapters I return to my roots, to the question of what we can do to cultivate the social field at the scale of the whole. This question has guided my entire journey—a journey that only now seems to finally have reached home.

# 6

# Upgrading Society's Operating System

When I talk to change makers, they all quickly agree on one thing. Even if their change initiative is wildly successful, the impact of their initiatives sooner or later hits a wall—the wall of the larger system.

Everyone understands that we will not overcome the challenges that we face today—the loss of our environment (to the ecological divide), of our society (to the social divide), and of our humanity (to the cultural-spiritual divide)—by adding one more initiative or idea to the mix.

To address these challenges, we need to step back and look at the bigger system. We need to **update the mental and structural operating code.** To use the language of smartphones, instead of just creating another app, we need to upgrade the entire operating system (OS). This chapter focuses on that larger narrative. How can we upgrade the economic, democratic, and educational operating systems in our societies? How can we make these systems sense and see themselves?

# Economy 4.0

In the spring of 2017, I attended a meeting convened by the DOEN Foundation in Amsterdam that brought together key innovators working on ways to forge a new economy. It was an intriguing microcosm of change makers and pioneers, each of whom was focused on a different leverage point: eco-system restoration, cradle-to-cradle design, social entrepreneurship, impact investing, tax reform, technology for good, the sharing economy, collaborative leadership, cooperatives, local currencies, and so on.

But two things were missing: first, a framework for linking all of these areas, and second, a shared mechanism for amplifying the new economic narrative as effectively as traditional media amplify the narrative of destruction that the old economy currently enacts.

What would this broader framework look like?

## The Root Issue: Commodity Fiction

There are many excellent examples of social entrepreneurship, socially responsible business, impact investing, and triple-bottom-line reporting. But most are focused primarily on symptoms, not structural root causes.

In his 1944 book *The Great Transformation,* political economist Karl Polanyi describes capitalism as a **commodity fiction.** Capitalism, or the market society, as he calls it, is constructed on the foundation of a fiction—namely that nature, labor, and money are commodities; they are produced for the marketplace, for consumption. But, Polanyi argues, nature is not a commodity. It is not produced by us for market consumption. Neither are human beings (labor). And neither is money. But in the market system all of these are treated *as if* they are commodities.

According to Polanyi, the result is phenomenal growth, but also massive negative externalities in the form of environmental destruction, poverty, and cyclical monetary breakdowns.

# The Solution: Update the Economic Operating System

Societies have responded to these dysfunctionalities by creating **institutional innovations** such as labor and environmental standards, social security, and the Federal Reserve System, in which market mechanisms are suspended where they are not useful.

Today, more than a century after the first upgrade of capitalism's operating system, we find ourselves once again confronted with challenges—but this time the challenges are global.

To respond to these challenges, we created an informal roundtable at MIT to think seriously about economics and prosperity in the light of the social and ecological challenges of our time. We looked at many key variables and concluded that, if they were leveraged simultaneously, the result would be an update of the economic operating system that could **shift our system from ego-to eco-system awareness.** I call these variables "acupuncture points" because they function like pressure points do on our bodies: When activated, they can have a regenerative impact on the whole system.

# The Matrix of Economic Transformation: Seven Acupuncture Points

These are the seven acupuncture points: **Nature, Labor,** and **Capital** (the three classical production factors); **Technology** and **Management** (the two more recent additions to the modern production function); **Consumption** (the user side of the equation); and **Governance** (how to coordinate the whole thing).

In all seven areas there are problem symptoms that call for reframing the deeper core issue (see figure 14). And for each one there are practical leverage points for transforming the current egocentric system into one that is eco-centric. Take a moment to contemplate the landscape depicted in figure 14 or, if you have an aversion to such tables, just continue reading.

| OS | NATURE | LABOR | CAPITAL |
|---|---|---|---|
| ISSUE | FINITE RESOURCES VS. INFINITE GROWTH | 40% OF JOBS GONE BY 2050 | DECOUPLING OF FINANCIAL AND REAL ECONOMY |
| REFRAME: FROM EGO TO ECO | FROM RESOURCE- TO ECO-SYSTEM | FROM JOBS TO ENTREPRENEUR- SHIP | FROM EXTRACTIVE TO INTENTIONAL CAPITAL |
| LEVERAGE POINT 1 | CIRCULAR ECONOMY | UNIVERSAL BASIC INCOME | CIRCULAR CURRENCIES |
| LEVERAGE POINT 2 | ECO-SYSTEM RESTORATION AND CIRCULAR AGRICULTURE | LEARNING TO ACTIVATE THE BEST POTENTIAL | TAXING RESOURCES INSTEAD OF LABOR |

FIGURE 14: The Matrix of Economic Transformation

An upgrade of the overall economic operating requires the following shifts.

## Nature: From Resource to Eco-system

The central challenge of our existing economic system is that it is based on the objective of infinite growth in a world of finite resources. Thus the task is to reframe nature as an eco-system rather than a resource. Instead of treating nature's gifts as commodities that we buy, use, and throw away, we must treat the natural world as a circular ecology that we need to cultivate and co-evolve with. Leverage points for shifting the system in this direction include:

| TECHNOLOGY | MANAGEMENT | CONSUMPTION | GOVERNANCE |
|---|---|---|---|
| DECOUPLING OF INNOVATION AND REAL NEEDS | MASSIVE INSTITUTIONAL LEADERSHIP FAILURE | DECOUPLING OF GDP AND WELL-BEING | DISCONNECT OF GOVERNANCE AND IMPACT ON STAKEHOLDERS |
| FROM CREATIVITY REDUCING TO CREATIVITY ENHANCING | FROM SILOS TO ECO-SYSTEM | FROM GDP AND CONSUMERISM TO GNH AND WELL-BEING | FROM HIERARCHY AND MARKETS TO ABC |
| TOOLS FOR VISUALIZING FOOTPRINT | INFRASTRUC-TURES FOR ECO-SYSTEM COORDINATION | NEW ECONOMIC PROGRESS INDICATORS | ECO-SYSTEM: MAKING THE SYSTEM SEE ITSELF |
| TOOLS FOR SEEING YOURSELF FROM THE WHOLE | MASSIVE FREE CAPACITY-BUILDING MECHANISMS | PARTICIPATORY BUDGETING | COMMONS-BASED OWNERSHIP RIGHTS |

- A circular economy with cradle-to-cradle design principles
- Eco-system restoration with circular agriculture that cultivates the soil

## Labor: From Doing a Job to Doing Your Own Thing

By 2050, it is estimated that roughly 40 percent of our current jobs will be replaced by automation. Instead of thinking of labor as a "job" that we perform to earn money, we must reinvent work and treat it as a creative act that allows us to realize our highest potential. Leverage points for shifting the future of work to a more interpersonal and cultural-creative realm include:

- Universal basic income for all
- Free access to education 4.0 that activates one's highest future potential

## Money: From Extractive to Intentional

We are all aware of the unprecedented accumulation of money on a global level. The challenge here is to redirect the flow of financial capital into the real economy and renew the societal commons. Today we have too much money in one place—speculative, extractive money—and too little money in another—intentional money that contributes to the regeneration of our ecological, social, and cultural commons. Leverage points for redesigning the flow of money include:

- Circular currencies, for replacing extractive money
- Tax system reform, for taxing resources instead of labor

## Technology: From Creativity-Reducing to Creativity-Enhancing

How can technology empower people to be makers and creators of their worlds and systems rather than being manipulated by tech companies like Facebook or Google? Both Facebook and Google started as idealistic student enterprises with the idea of making the world a better place. And in many ways they did. But as they grew, they also abandoned their original stance against advertising in order to satisfy their investors' desire to maximize their gain. And now we learn that these same tech companies, perhaps inadvertently, played a significant role in helping the Russian government and other vested interests to manipulate the 2016 U.S. election. This is just one example of how quickly technology, if not used with a very clear ethical intention, can turn from a force for good to a force that supports various shady anti-democratic and anti-constitutional interests.

Leverage points for new co-creative social technologies include:
- Tools that allow individuals and communities to visualize the

social-ecological footprint of their consumption choices at the point of purchase.

- Technology-enabled tools that let individuals and communities see themselves through the mirror of the whole. (Remember the story of the German healthcare group in chapter 5 and shown in figure 12; with smart technologies this shift in consciousness could happen on a much bigger scale.)

## Leadership

We collectively create results that nobody wants (that is, the destruction of nature, of society, and of our humanity). The challenge here is to counteract massive leadership failure across institutions and sectors. Instead of pandering to super-egos, we need to strengthen leaders' capacity to co-sense and co-shape the future on the level of the whole eco-system. Leverage points for moving in this direction include:

- Infrastructures for co-sensing: seeing the system from the edges (walking in the shoes of the most marginalized members) and from the whole (e.g.,

dialogue and Social Prensencing Theater)
- Large-scale capacity-building mechanisms that support ego-to-eco shifts (e.g., u.lab)

## Consumption

The challenge here is to develop well-being for all. Today, more output, more consumption, and more GDP does not translate into more well-being and happiness. Rather than promoting consumerism and metrics like gross domestic product, we must implement sharing-economy practices and measurements of well-being such as gross national happiness (GNH) or the genuine progress indicator (GPI). Leverage points in this domain include:
- Well-being-economy practices and new economic indicators
- Participatory budgeting

## Governance

The challenge here is to close the disconnect between decision making in complex systems and the lived experiences of people affected by those decisions. Reinventing governance means complementing the three classic coordination mechanisms that we are familiar with (the visible hand of hierarchy, the invisible hand of the markets, and the multi-centric coordination among organized interest groups) with a **fourth mechanism: acting from shared awareness of the whole.** Leverage points in this domain include:

- Infrastructures that make it possible for **the system to sense and see itself** in order to catalyze awareness-based collective action (ABC)
- Commons-based owner ship rights that protect the rights of future generations (in addition to private and public property rights)

# A Roadmap for the Ego-to-Eco Shift

Stepping back and looking at the bigger picture, what do we see? Each leverage point addresses what Polanyi articulated as the commodity fiction of nature, labor, and money, but from a different angle.

To summarize: By looking at the economy through the Theory U lens, we can identify ways to upgrade the operating system along all seven acupuncture points. Details about how to implement the matrix of economic evolution can be found in the book *Leading from the Emerging Future: From Ego-system to Eco-system Economies,* which I wrote with Katrin Kaufer, and on the interactive multimedia hub that we are co-creating with HuffPost (at www.presencing.org).

What will it take to make all of this work? Political will. Which brings us to the next topic.

# Democracy 4.0

Our current democratic system is broken in many places, not only in the United States, where that condition is perhaps most visible. But what is the under lying problem? The lack of an evolving democratic system. Historically, the democratic system has evolved from:

> 1.0: one-party democracy (centralized), to

2.0: multi-party, indirect (parliamentary) democracy, to

3.0: participatory indirect (parliamentary) democracy, to a possible

4.0: participatory direct, distributed, digital, dialogic (4D) democracy.

Many people have written about these topics, so let us just look at the big picture.

The United States (with the rise of Trumpism), the United Kingdom (Brexit), Turkey (Erdogan), Russia (Putin), and the Philippines (Duterte) share one thing in common: All operate with a 2.0 or 3.0 democracy that seems incapable of addressing many of these nations' challenges. Voters in these countries have therefore expressed their frustrations with the status quo by voting for outliers who would disrupt the establishment, even by taking democracy backward. People's frustrations have created a stage from which these leaders could advocate for a more authoritarian system (1.0 "democracy"). What was largely missing from these countries' elections was a future-oriented alternative: ideas for a 4.0 democracy that would shift the source of power from special interest groups to the real needs of communities, from a top-down leadership to a more shared process of co-sensing and co-shaping.

We do see democracy 4.0 in some cities and other place-based urban and rural communities, where conversations are more direct, more distributed (collective), more digital (online-to-offline), and more dialogic, by which I mean conversations that allow the system to see itself.

The media have a key role to play in the shift to a 4.0 democracy. Maintaining a democracy without in dependent media is like trying to breathe without oxygen. You may be busy grabbing for air, but the effort is not doing you any good. It will bring down the system. The current problem with our media is twofold: there is too much dependence on special interests and too much focus on the *absencing* rather than the *presencing* side of the equation.

# Cross-Sector 4.0

The disruptions in this century so far are symptoms of three deeper structural problems:

- The inability to generate well-being for all (the economic divide)
- The inability to generate real participation for all (the political divide)
- The inability to create generative learning opportunities for all (the cultural divide)

A comprehensive restructuring will require us to rethink and redesign the following interrelated systems that usually are thought of as separate: health, education, food, and finance. A fifth system, restructuring of management and governance, would be needed to coordinate the whole. What would it take to reimagine these systems from a *presencing* lens—that is, through the activation of generative social fields?

Today, the global food system is still profoundly destructive. The health system is still sick. The education system is unable to learn. The global financial system is heading full throttle into the next crash. Foundations and philanthropists still place their assets in the old economy, thereby aggravating the root problems that their grantees are supposed to remedy. The green, sustainable, and socially responsible innovators in all these spaces are stuck in the niches that first gave them space to develop something new. But now these niches are increasingly crowded with mainstream players who adopt the new labels and sound bites while often perpetuating old models. For example, Amazon's acquisition of Whole Foods will likely do to organics what Uber did to the sharing economy: Take something that was born out of a different economic logic (a grocery store dedicated to healthy food) and reshape it to fit into an economic operating system that is firmly based in the old paradigm—a paradigm that aims for world domination.

Each of these systems has already begun the shift toward 4.0 (see figure 15). But how can we develop, support, and maintain the momentum for what must be a vast transformation of systems?

## Health: From Pathogenesis to Salutogenesis

Realizing that only 20 percent of health depends on the provision of healthcare services while 60 percent depends on social, environmental, and behavioral factors, major health system innovators like Kaiser Permanente have begun to refocus from *pathogenesis,* treating the symptoms of illness, to *salutogenesis,* strengthening the social determinants of health and well-being in communities.

Mainstream health organizations have transformed from:

- OS 1.0, traditional **input-centric** operations, revolving around doctors and healthcare institutions, to
- OS 2.0, **output-centric,** revolving around evidence-based, standards-based, and science-centric ways of operating, to

| OS | HEALTH | LEARNING |
|---|---|---|
| **1.0:** INPUT AND AUTHORITY-CENTRIC | TRADITIONAL DOCTOR-CENTRIC MEDICINE | TRADITIONAL TEACHER-CENTRIC |
| **2.0:** OUTPUT AND EFFICIENCY-CENTRIC | EVIDENCE-BASED MEDICINE | TESTING-CENTRIC |
| **3.0:** STAKEHOLDER AND CUSTOMER-CENTRIC | PATIENT-CENTRIC MEDICINE | LEARNER-CENTRIC |
| **4.0:** GENERATIVE ECO-SYSTEM-CENTRIC | SALUTOGENESIS: STRENGTHENING SOURCES OF WELL-BEING | CO-CREATIVE: ACTIVATE DEEPER SOURCES OF LEARNING |

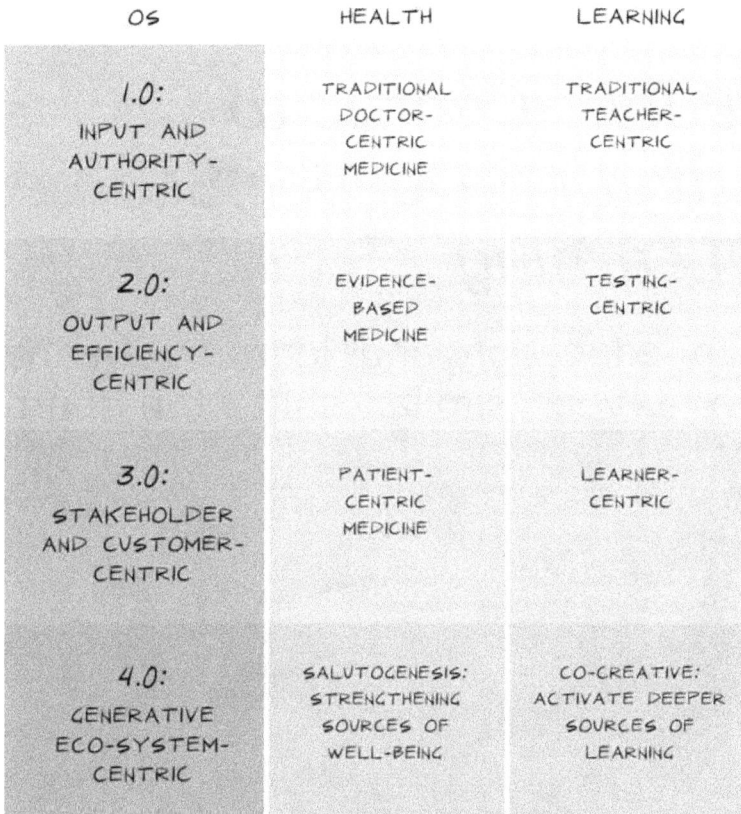

FIGURE 15: Four Stages of Systems Evolution, Four Operating Systems

- OS 3.0, **patient-centric** experiences for organizing more seamless and innovative ways of providing healthcare services, until finally, real innovators are now moving, to
- OS 4.0, **strengthening the sources of health** and **well-being** (salutogenesis).

# Education: From Student-Centric to Activating Deeper Sources of Learning

In education and learning we have seen a very similar shift, the journey from:

| FARM/FOOD | FINANCE | GOVERNANCE |
|---|---|---|
| TRADITIONAL FARMER-CENTRIC | TRADITIONAL FINANCIAL CAPITAL | HIERARCHY |
| INDUSTRIAL MONO-CULTURES | EXTRACTIVE CAPITAL: WALL STREET | COMPETITION |
| ORGANIC: ECO-CENTRIC | RESPONSIBLE CAPITAL: IMPACT INVESTING | STAKEHOLDER DIALOGUES |
| CULTIVATING SOURCES OF ECO-SOCIAL RENEWAL | GENERATIVE CAPITAL: SYSTEMS TRANSFORMATION | ABC: AWARENESS-BASED COLLECTIVE ACTION |

- OS 1.0, **input-centric** operations, revolving around traditional teaching and teachers, to
- OS 2.0, **output-centric,** revolving around standardized curricula and teaching for testing (i.e., bulimia learning—fast in, fast out), to
- OS 3.0, **learner-centric,** which puts the experience of the student at the center of reshaping learning environments, to
- OS 4.0, connecting learners with the **sources of creativity** and the deepest essence of our humanity, while teaching them to co-sense emerging future possibilities and bring them to fruition. The most innovative schools (and in Finland the whole school system) are experimenting with 4.0 education and learning.

# Food: From Organics to Living Eco-system Presence

In the agriculture and food sector, there has been a shift from:
- OS 1.0, **traditional** ways of farming, to

- OS 2.0, science-based **industrial agriculture,** to
- OS 3.0 model of **sustainable farming practices,** to
- OS 4.0 agriculture that goes way beyond food production by cultivating farms as places of economic, ecological, social, and spiritual-cultural renewal—healing the living ecosystems.

We know now that the industrial Ag 2.0 model with its focus on monocultures, maximized output, and profitability has been a disaster not only for the planet (soil erosion, water pollution) but also for people (farmers, workers, supply chains, consumers). Many of the innovators in the organic Ag 3.0 space are now, after first successes, worried and/or frustrated. They built brands. They built responsible supply chains. They built communities. But below the surface questions loom: How do we survive massive digitization, big data, and companies like Monsanto that make a billion dollar business out of destroying the integrity of farms as living eco-systems? Plus, what really is organic? Just a smaller footprint? Or is it something more and, if so, more of what? These questions point to an emerging 4.0 model that focuses on closing the feedback loop not only across the ecological divide (through circular agriculture), but also across the social divide (through inclusive supply chains), and the spiritual divide (by cultivating the eco-presence of farms as space for societal renewal).

## *Finance: From Extractive to Generative Capital*

The evolution of finance and money is deeply interconnected with our current systemic "stuckness" in 2.0 and 3.0 systems. The mainstream financial system has moved from:

- OS 1.0, the model of **traditional** person-centric banking, to
- OS 2.0 practices of commodity-centric banking, with **extractive capital** that is blind to externalities (the Wall Street "big six"), until we now see a worldwide awakening to the fact that these financial practices are a path to self-destruction, setting the stage for

- OS 3.0, **impact investing** and more responsible use of money—that is, more awareness of the positive and negative externalities. Most foundations, impact investors, and venture philanthropists share these ideas and goals. Still, their projects and programs rarely address the root causes of our failing systems, which brings us to

- OS 4.0, **generative capital,** defined by an intentional focus on the longer-term impact and on regenerating the creative, social, and ecological commons. Why did Whole Foods get sold to Amazon? For the same reason Seventh Generation got sold to Unilever: because the investors wanted to see the money—in other words, because the intention of the capital owners focused on extraction, not on serving the long-term impact on the whole. Which brings us to governance.

## Governance: From Competition to ABC

# (Awareness-based Collective Action)

Historically, the 1.0 mechanism was hierarchy and centralization; the 2.0 mechanism came with the rise of markets and competition; and the 3.0 mechanism took the form of negotiation among organized stakeholder groups.

The most important and least understood institutional innovation today concerns the creation of a 4.0 coordination mechanism that is based on making the system sense and see itself: awareness-based collective action (ABC)—that is, acting from seeing the whole. Today we see the first examples of this mechanism in governance being adopted at the local level. In many cities and local communities, stakeholders are collaborating to rebuild the environmental, social, political, and cultural commons. But what is missing is an understanding of how this collaboration across boundaries can be aggregated and extended to larger systems—regions, countries, and continents. That is where the principles and practices of chapter 5 may have their highest relevance.

# 4.0 Lab

In the summer of 2017 I visited the family farm near Hamburg where I grew up. (It is, by the way, no longer just a family farm, as we turned the owner ship over to a foundation committed to bridging the three divides.) The purpose of my visit was to attend a meeting of founders and CEOs of green brands in Europe and Asia. Many of the major green pioneers and innovators sat in the meeting circle. It was an eye-opening conversation that taught me many things about the evolution of the food sector.

Looking into that circle, it was also clear to me that what made those leaders (and their companies) so successful in the 3.0 world will not help them succeed in the emerging 4.0 environment. And all of them knew that.

Seeing that, I explored an idea with the group. I proposed setting up a global innovation lab that would bring together pioneers and leading innovators from all four of the systems I just described—food, finance, health, and learning—to focus on cocreating a cross-sector 4.0 innovation lab.

In broad outline, the "4.0 Lab" would begin with regional labs in one or multiple geographies. Each regional lab would start with an agenda-setting workshop in which the key innovators and institutional partners would connect, get to know each other, and co-initiate the agenda and set the regional focus of each lab. The Presencing Institute would support these labs with methods and tools, as well as with our online-to-offline u.lab platform, and share the results via the joint multimedia platform on the new economy that we jointly curate with HuffPost.

Even though this idea came up only toward the end of the meeting, three or four of the founders in the circle instantly said "I'm in"—even without knowing exactly what they are in for. Nor of course do I. But I do believe that these kinds of cross-sectoral initiatives are needed now more than ever—in many places, regions, and geographies—because no one can create 4.0 platforms and eco-systems alone.

7

# Returning to the Roots

I started my journey on a farm. One day when I was five or six years old, a family friend visited. He worked in the state government in Hamburg. I was transfixed by the stories he shared about a world that was completely foreign to me and remember wondering if someday I might be connected to the world he operated in.

## With Compliments to the East German KGB

Later, of course, I became very interested in what was happening in the outside world and got involved as an activist in various social movements. During the heyday of the peace movement in Europe, I occasionally traveled back and forth between East and West Germany—until one day in 1984, when I found myself on a black list. I was barred from entering East Germany.

Then, in 1989, the Berlin Wall came down. In 1990 the German government formed the Stasi Records Agency, which gave German citizens access to the files the Stasi (the East German equivalent of the Soviet KGB) had kept on them. Of course, I was curious to find out what was in my file. When I saw it, I was amazed how little they knew about me (we had overestimated their proficiency). The files had a very German bureaucratic structure. Each one included a section that described its subject and his or her activities. In my case they wrote, "He inspires leading circles of the opposition movement." Wow, I thought. They had condensed to a single sentence what would have taken me days to describe! I would not have made that claim myself, but looking back, perhaps I have in some small moments been lucky to embody elements of that description.

Needless to say, those same words could be used to describe what I am still trying to do today. "Inspires" means mobilizing action from within; "leading circles" means collective leadership, not just a bunch of individuals; and "movement" refers to awareness-based change, something much deeper than just tinkering with institutional structures. So I owe a thank-you to whoever wrote that description in my Stasi file. It did not change my purpose. But it brought more clarity to it.

# Staying on Course

When I was younger, many people told me, "Just wait until you get older, then all your ideas about change will fade and your priorities will shift." As if what I felt in my heart was something like a childhood illness that I should leave behind as I grew up. Whenever I heard statements like that I would shrug and look noncommittal, but inside I was thinking, "*Nooo!* No way! What are these people talking about?"

Today I probably feel as connected to imminent societal change as I ever have. Maybe it is because of the moment in history we are living in. Or maybe it is because of my age. My body is getting older but, oddly, my energy seems to be getting younger. It feels as if my past life was a preparation for the real thing, which is about to begin. What is that real thing? I cannot say exactly. But I can feel it. It is about the current moment in our communities—about what I feel wants to happen in so many places right now.

## "I Can't Not Do It"

One of my most important teachers was the peace researcher Johan Galtung. When I first heard him lecture at the Free University of Berlin in 1983, it was if a light turned on in my mind: Suddenly I knew what action science could look like. It was science that went into the field, that participated in the trenches of advancing societal change.

The next year, as a student at Witten/Herdecke University, I invited Galtung to a student-led conference. Long story short, he ended up spending more than fifteen years there as a visiting professor. Each term he would come for a couple of weeks and stay in the guest room of "The Villa," a crumbling old house that a fellow student and I had rented for a dozen of our classmates. The Villa was for many years a place that felt like the heart of the community of learners and teachers at that small, startup university. One day, Galtung and the dean of our department were there having breakfast with us. Galtung, known for his theory of structural violence, had taught at universities in many cultures. One student turned to him and asked, "Johan, having accomplished all that you have, what's left for you now? What is it that you want to create in the remaining years of your life?" He responded, "I have an idea for a mobile global peace university. Its students would travel the world learning how to see society as a living whole and viewing it from the perspectives of different cultures and civilizations."

When he started to describe in more detail what that global learning journey would look like, I knew instantly that this was what I was meant to do. Katrin and others at the table that morning had the same feeling—*I can't not do it!* That deep knowing was a source of enormous energy. As it turned out, Galtung had tried to create such a global peace university project at the U.S.-based Bard College. But the complexity of organizing, financing, and managing it had proved too much. Although as students we lacked any experience in such matters, we knew in our guts that we could do it. And then we did—in record time.

Five of us pulled it together in just a few months: We mapped out the project, raised half a million dollars from industry and private sponsors, contracted with twelve partner universities and 290 lecturers, recruited 35 students from ten different countries, including Eastern Europe, and raised money for scholarships. We knew that once we embarked on this journey, no setback (of which there were several) would stop us from getting there. Later, Galtung compared our way of operating to a seek-and-destroy missile: "Once you lock on to the target, you don't stop until you hit it—even if the target moves."

Although I wished he had used a different analogy, what he said still rings true. Whenever I sense that feeling of "locking on," I know that one way or another we are going to succeed. The locking on, however, is not directed from the head. It emerges from your whole being as you and the core group lean into the field of the future.

There is one area, though, where this "locking on" experience has not yet produced too many tangible results. For decades I have had a larger vision of creating a global awareness-based action research university for societal transformation. Yet, despite the sense of possibility, a pathway to bringing this into reality never appeared. Then, in 2015, when I was about to give up on this aspiration or dream, something unexpected happened. The u.lab—the global MOOC—came along. And suddenly there it was: a pathway to that decades-long intention.

# u.lab

The u.lab does to the global social field what the organic farmer does to the agricultural field: it cultivates the soil. In the case of u.lab we do this in the form of an online-to-offline learning platform that links, connects, and capacitates change makers from 185 countries. It is part of an emerging global innovation ecology of change makers that cultivate generative social fields to evolve our economic, democratic, and educational systems. We as u.lab and PI support these initiatives by focusing on these four core activities (see figure 16):

- **Co-convening innovation labs** that bring together key players from all three sectors (business, government, civil society)—as outlined in chapter 5
- **Pioneering massive capacity-building mechanisms** that integrate the intelligences of the head, heart, and hand—as exemplified in u.lab
- **Knowledge creation** that links action research and systems thinking from the viewpoint of an evolving human consciousness—as spelled out throughout this book
- **Activating movements** and generative social fields through new

narratives of economic, democratic, and civilizational renewal—as outlined in chapter 6

An outgrowth of the MIT Learning Center, the Presencing Institute (PI) and its global network of practitioners have successfully prototyped the above elements across sectors and systems, including labs, tools, and online-to-offline capacity-building platforms. Yet we have not even started to reach the level of impact and scale that we sense is possible and called for now.

The journey since the first MOOC in 2015 has been a revelation to us because, for the first time, we have seen a platform and community go to a massive scale very quickly. The spontaneous emergence of 500–600 hubs—self-organized, place-based communities—across cities, countries, and cultures opened our eyes to the urgent need to connect people and purpose in more fluid, personal, practical, and self-organizing ways.

CREATING
KNOWLEDGE
CROSS-
DISCIPLINE:
Science,
Consciousness,
Action Research

CONVENING
INNOVATION LABS
CROSS-
SECTOR:
Business
Government
Civil Society

BUILDING
CAPACITY
CROSS-
INTELLIGENCES:
Open Mind
Open Heart
Open Will

ACTIVATING GENERATIVE SOCIAL FIELDS

NARRATIVES FOR CIVILIZATIONAL RENEWAL

FIGURE 16: U.SCHOOL: A Global Action
Research University in the Making

We have also seen larger institutions
begin to utilize u.lab, including

companies, NGOs, and the governments of Scotland and Netherlands. Kenneth Hogg, director for innovation in the government of Scotland, explains why the Scottish government is using u.lab: **"The world is changing rapidly and we cannot predict the future. We need a new capacity, to make sense of what is going on and of what a collective response could be. That capacity is sensemaking, which is not analysis, since it is using a broader range of data and sources of information. U.lab helps to develop this capacity to make sense of what is happening around us and to sense into future possibilities to do things differently."**

As of this writing, we are at a unique juncture where this work could very quickly advance, evolve, and grow to significant global impact—and we're taking many steps, building our institutional infrastructure and upgrading our technological platforms in preparation. If you feel inspired to participate, the latest news and updates will always be posted on the Presencing Institute website.

To keep the global heartbeat of the community going, we are in the process of creating a hybrid between media and movement building including monthly live sessions online, in which the larger community can connect, share case stories, engage in small group dialogue, and use global mindfulness moments for cultivating the soil of the collective.

Even though many of the stories of this book revolve around my own experiences, I do not think they are in any way unique. In fact, the very reason for writing this book is my belief that the kind of stories it shares are much more widely experienced across sectors, systems, cultures, and communities than most people understand. They belong to a larger pattern of awakening and movement building that many people sense and begin to tune in to.

Forty years ago, my home burned to the ground. Today it is the world that is on fire. If I have learned anything from my grandfather and from the various experiences of disruption, it is this: When disruption happens, there are two options:

- You can turn away, close down, and move toward **absencing:** enacting prejudice, hate, and fear; or
- You can open up and turn toward **presencing:** embodying curiosity, compassion, and courage.

Those two responses are less than an inch apart in my mind. It is our intentional act to choose the latter that changes the way the future unfolds. Action from shared awareness redirects the course of our collective journey. It holds the seeds of a future that stays in need of us. Every moment. Now.

# Get Involved

If this speaks to you, here are three actions you can take to deepen your exploration, connection, and participation in this movement of awareness-based systems change:

1. Join the growing number of people who collaborate at the intersection of science, consciousness and social change by visiting www.presencing .org, and creating a profile.

2. Enroll in the free u.lab 1x to gain access to Theory U-based methods and networks.

3. Put the next upcoming live session on your calendar, and join the conversation.

The offerings on www.presencing.org are continually evolving and changing. Check back often for the latest updates, and share the resources with friends and colleagues. And most importantly, put what you've learned here and through the website, into action in your own local context, and share back what you learn about leading profound change. That, ultimately, is truly how this movement will grow.

# About the Author

Dr. C. Otto Scharmer is a senior lecturer at MIT and co-founder of the Presencing Institute. Scharmer introduced the concept of *"presencing"*—learning from the emerging future—in his bestselling books *Theory U* and *Presence* (the latter co-authored with Peter Senge, Joseph Jaworski, and Betty Sue Flowers).

In 2015 he co-founded the MITx u.lab, a massive open online course for leading profound change that has since activated a global eco-system of societal and personal renewal involving more than 100,000 users from 185 countries. With his colleagues he has facilitated innovation labs on reinventing business, finance, education, health, and government across cultures.

Otto received the Jamieson Prize for Excellence in Teaching at MIT (2015) and the European Leonardo Corporate Learning Award (2016). His vision is to create a global action research university for societal transformation that integrates science, consciousness, and social change.

For more information visit www.otto scharmer.com.

# About the Presencing Institute

The Presencing Institute was founded in 2006 by MIT's Otto Scharmer and colleagues in order to create an action research platform at the intersection of science, spirituality, and social change. Over the past two decades, we have developed Theory U as a social technology, led cross-sector change initiatives worldwide, and created a popular innovation platform (originally launched as a massive open online course) called u.lab.

Today, in an effort to cultivate and activate generative social fields, our practitioners, facilitators, and action researchers, worldwide, engage in four intersecting activities:

1. *Innovation Labs:* Co-convene stakeholders from business, government, and civil society to collectively respond to the disruptive challenges of our time.
2. *Capacity Building:* Develop collective capacity for leading profound innovation and change by linking

the intelligences of the head, heart, and hand.

3.  *Action Research:* Capture knowledge and refine Theory U – based social technologies, and develop methods for making visible the deep structures of social fields.

4.  *Movement Building:* Shift public consciousness from reactive to generative by building free educational platforms where people can discover and link around new narratives of economic, democratic, and civilizational renewal.

For more information about the Presencing Institute, please visit www.p resencing.org.

Also by Otto Scharmer
**Theory U**
**Leading from the Future as It Emerges, Second Edition**

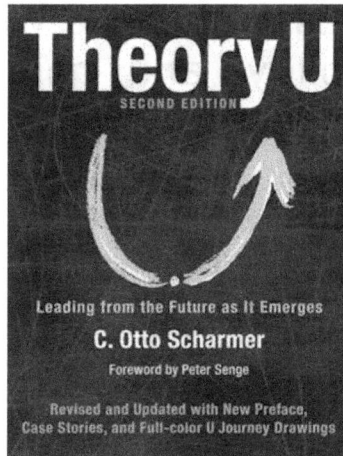

In this groundbreaking book, Otto Scharmer shows how, by moving through his U process, we can consciously access the blind spot—the inner place from which attention and intention originate. This enables us to connect to our authentic Self—the deepest source of knowledge and inspiration—in the realm of "presencing," a term coined by Scharmer that combines the concepts of presence and sensing. *Theory U* is based on ten years of research and action learning and interviews with over 150 practitioners and thought leaders. It offers a rich diversity of compelling stories and examples and includes dozens of exercises and practices that allow leaders, and entire organizations, to shift awareness, connect with the best future possibility, and gain the ability to realize it.

**BK** Berrett–Koehler Publishers, Inc.
*www.bkconnection.com*

By Otto Scharmer and Katrin Kaufer
## Leading from the Emerging Future
## From Ego-System to Eco-System Economies

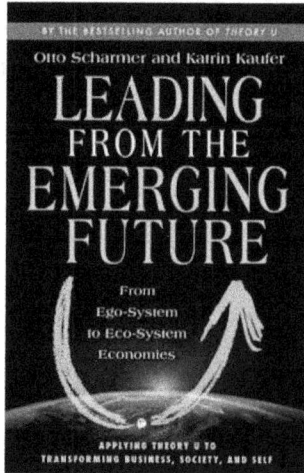

We have entered an age of disruption. Financial collapse, climate change, resource depletion, and a growing gap between rich and poor are but a few of the signs. Otto Scharmer and Katrin Kaufer ask, why do we collectively create results nobody wants? Meeting the challenges of this century requires updating our economic logic and operating system from an obsolete "ego-system" focused entirely on the well-being of oneself to an eco-system awareness that emphasizes the well-being of the whole. Scharmer and Kaufer take readers on a thought-provoking journey filled with real-world examples that will help leaders and change makers transform and renew business, society, and the self and create a new economy that is more resilient, intentional, inclusive, and aware.

Berrett–Koehler Publishers, Inc.
*www.bkconnection.com*

**Berrett–Koehler**
BK Publishers

**Berrett-Koehler** is an independent publisher dedicated to an ambitious mission: *Connecting people and ideas to create a world that works for all.*

We believe that the solutions to the world's problems will come from all of us, working at all levels: in our organizations, in our society, and in our own lives. Our BK Business books help people make their organizations more humane, democratic, diverse, and effective (we don't think there's any contradiction there). Our BK Currents books offer pathways to creating a more just, equitable, and sustainable society. Our BK Life books help people create positive change in their lives and align their personal practices with their aspirations for a better world.

All of our books are designed to bring people seeking positive change together around the ideas that empower them to see and shape the world in a new way.

And we strive to practice what we preach. At the core of our approach is

Stewardship, a deep sense of responsibility to administer the company for the benefit of all of our stakeholder groups including authors, customers, employees, investors, service providers, and the communities and environment around us. Everything we do is built around this and our other key values of quality, partnership, inclusion, and sustainability.

This is why we are both a B-Corporation and a California Benefit Corporation—a certification and a for-profit legal status that require us to adhere to the highest standards for corporate, social, and environmental performance.

We are grateful to our readers, authors, and other friends of the company who consider themselves to be part of the BK Community. We hope that you, too, will join us in our mission.

# A BK Business Book

We hope you enjoy this BK Business book. BK Business books pioneer new leadership and management practices and socially responsible approaches to business. They are designed to provide you with groundbreaking and practical tools to transform your work and organizations while upholding the triple bottom line of people, planet, and profits. High-five!

To find out more, visit www.bkconnection.com.

**Berrett–Koehler**
BK Publishers

Connecting people and ideas
to create a world that works for all

Dear Reader,

Thank you for picking up this book and joining our worldwide community of Berrett-Koehler readers. We share ideas that bring positive change into people's lives, organizations, and society.

**To welcome you, we'd like to offer you a free e-book.** You can pick from among twelve of our bestselling books by entering the promotional code **BKP92E** here: http://www.bkconnection.com/welcome.

When you claim your free e-book, we'll also send you a copy of our e-newsletter, the *BK Communiqué.* Although you're free to unsubscribe, there are many benefits to sticking around. In every issue of our newsletter you'll find
- A free e-book
- Tips from famous authors
- Discounts on spotlight titles
- Hilarious insider publishing news

- A chance to win a prize for answering a riddle

Best of all, our readers tell us, "Your newsletter is the only one I actually read." So claim your gift today, and please stay in touch!

Sincerely,

Charlotte Ashlock
Steward of the BK Website

Questions? Comments? Contact me at bkcommunity@bkpub.com.

Certified

Ⓑ

Corporation
bcorporation.net

# Z